◻ Table of Contents ◻

Welcome to your *Lioness Arising Safari Guide*! I'm thrilled you've joined me for this journey. I pray it will be interactive, fun, and empowering, because many hours have been poured into this project. It is my prayer that vision will be quickened and the truth of who and whose you are will come alive and transform you and the members of the "pride" you gather with.

This *Safari Guide* contains eleven chapters, which correspond with the eleven book chapters and the eight video and audio teaching sessions.

FEATURES TO LOOK FOR IN EACH CHAPTER:

❖ **Scriptures** – profound passages from the Word to transform your life

❖ **Legend Lioness** – words of wisdom from history-shaping women

❖ **Hunt Quest** – questions designed to challenge you to action

❖ **Pride Play** – activities for you and your pride of sisters

❖ **Lioness Lessons** – highlighted "power points" from each chapter

❖ **Pride Purpose** – further identification of the lioness in you

❖ **Prowess** – key statements to help define and develop your personal prowess

❖ **Fierce Facts** – fun and interesting facts about lions and lionesses

❖ **Prayer Roar** – life-changing prayers that activate what was awakened in the chapter

❖ **Impressions** – your personal reflections

Throughout the *Safari Guide*, you will also discover definitions and other inspirational quotes from influential leaders. *(Note: Celebrating one's moments of inspiration and brilliance does not equate to endorsing one's entire life. Pause a moment and lean into the world of a man or woman who has gone before you in time.)*

Some helpful pointers...

Begin and end each of your study sessions with prayer. Invite the Holy Spirit to teach you and lead you into all truth (see John 16:13).

Read the chapter(s) in the Lioness Arising book, complete the chapter(s) in this *Safari Guide,* and watch the corresponding DVD session—in that order.

Book and Safari Guide Chapter(s)	Video Session
Chapters 1-2	Session 1: Awaken a Lioness | A Force Unseen
Chapter 3	Session 2: Dangerously Awake
Chapter 4	Session 3: The Sum of Fear & Wonder
Chapter 5	Session 4: Strength Is for Service
Chapter 6	Session 5: Under the Same Mission
Chapters 7-8	Session 6: Greet & Groom | Lionesses Are Strategic
Chapter 9	Session 7: Lionesses Live in the Light & Hunt in the Dark
Chapters 10-11	Session 8: Walking & Roaring with Our Lion

Be consistent in your study. Whatever time and place you choose to do the study, stick to it. If you fall behind, don't quit. Push through to the finish. Your efforts will be rewarded.

Be honest as you answer each question. There are no wrong answers except those that are dishonest. Knowing the truth of God's Word, along with the truth about yourself, will bring freedom to your life that can be found no other way.

The material contained in this *Safari Guide* is life-transforming because it is the Word of God. It will change and challenge you to the degree you allow it. It is my prayer that through this safari you will be truly awakened to rise up and realize all you were created to be!

Most Sincerely,

Lisa

AWAKEN A LIONESS 1

Welcome to the pride, my lovely lioness sister. I hope you know you're loved already. This is a gathering and study constructed with you in mind.

As I typed I was again struck with the desperate need for a vehicle that intimately interacted with material in the book. It would be impossible to attempt this study without the *Lioness Arising* book.

I didn't want to label this a Bible study, nor did I want this to be a work-book. It is a guided safari into the wild *you*. You should know from the start that safaris are potentially dangerous. The truth is that I want the way you've thought and lived to be endangered. I want the enemy to know you are dangerous to his schemes. I want you to look deep inside yourself and find the fierce you.

Dangerous journeys are undertaken in the company of armed rangers who have navigated the trails before. Some of these plains I have walked, but others are uncharted territory.

I pray that you have found some lioness sisters to journey these paths with; but lovely one, if you haven't, please know you are not alone. Ultimately it is the Holy Spirit of the Most High God who will teach you, and my words will guide you through the tall grass and open plains until you are revealed radiant on the other side.

> Write down some of your goals for this study. This should be your expectation of what you hope to realize.
>
> _____
>
> _____
>
> _____
>
> _____
>
> _____

Understand that on a safari, different people notice different things. Some people are taken with the stature and swagger of the elephants while others notice the stunning stealth of the leopard. On any given day a new wonder and response might unfold. It is my prayer that all would see what they seek.

When on a safari, you are always on the lookout. It is my prayer that this journey is undertaken so that you might recover your vision. As exciting as having *a vision* sounds, it is more crucial that you be a person *of vision*. I believe it is quite possible that the only reason I *had a vision* was because God wanted to inspire you to be a daughter *of vision*.

In keeping with this pursuit, more than anything else, this first chapter is designed to reconnect you with the dynamic of vision. At the outset I want you to settle that God wants you to have clarity of vision and the ability to write it down.

"Writing is an exploration. You start from nothing and learn as you go."
E.L. Doctorow, American author & editor

It is my hope that through these pages we will honestly explore our relationship with God, ourselves, and each other.

In the beginning God spoke to Abraham, Jacob, and the prophets of old in visions. Throughout the New Testament God again spoke to His people through visions. (Peter, Cornelius, and Paul to name a few.) Then the Bible closes with the book of Revelation, which is John's vision to help God's people recover both their vision and perspective. It is also apparent that visions and dreams is a language in which God likes to speak to His children.

Nature itself is a tool of vision. It is a constant expression of God's vision to see us free.

To begin, let's interact with Emerson's quote:

> *"Cherish your visions and your dreams as they are the children of your soul; the blueprints of your ultimate achievements."*[2]
> Napoleon Hill, devout Christian & American author (1883-1970)

> *"Nature is made to conspire with spirit to emancipate us."*
> Ralph Waldo Emerson

1 |. What outdoor natural environment is your favorite? (If you need help, remember back to when you were young.)

Forest	Beach	Mountains	Streams
Desert	Lake	Open plains	_____

Sometimes I must look outside to recover the perspective of my life inside. Discovery happens outside of our control in environments beyond our making.

a. What sights inspire you?

Sunset	Sunrise	Clouds	Birds soaring
Lightning	A baby	A flower	_____

b. What creature pulls on you? (For an example, when I was young I wanted to be a dolphin.)

_____

_____

c. Which creature do you find the most frightening?

_____

_____

d. What sound of nature or music moves you? What does it awaken?

_____

_____

_____

e. What outdoor smells do you love?

_____

_____

_____

f. How do these invite you to break your bonds?

_____

_____

_____

Can you believe God laid each of these (and much more) out with fore-thought to awaken you? All of creation is set up to reveal the majesty and purpose of our God.

> Royal splendor radiates from him,
> A powerful beauty sets him apart.
> Bravo, God, Bravo!
> Everyone join in the great shout: Encore!
> In awe before the beauty, in awe before the might.
> Bring gifts and celebrate,
> Bow before the beauty of God,
> Then to your knees—everyone worship!
> Get out the message—God Rules!
> He put the world on a firm foundation;
> He treats everyone fair and square.
> Let's hear it from Sky,
> With Earth joining in,
> And a huge round of applause from Sea.

Let Wilderness turn cartwheels,
Animals, come dance,
Put every tree of the forest in the choir—
An extravaganza before God as he comes,
As he comes to set everything right on earth,
Set everything right, treat everyone fair.

Psalm 96:6-13

All creation celebrates God's salvation and justice; how can we do anything less? Therefore the whole purpose of this chapter is to enlarge your sight and open up your life to all God has for you.

☒ HUNT QUEST ☒

2 | Define the word *vision*:

_____
_____
_____
_____
_____
_____

Legend Lioness

"The most pathetic person in the world is someone who has sight, but has no vision."[3]

Helen Keller

Define the word *dream*:

_____
_____
_____

3 | In light of these definitions, have you ever had a vision or a dream? Write it, draw it, or record the words associated with it here:

_____
_____
_____

_____
_____
_____
_____

4 | Have you ever experienced the tangible presence of God?
_____

   a. If so, what was happening or what were you doing when this happened?
     _____
     _____
     _____

5 | When I relayed the vision of the lioness, could you see it?
_____
_____

   a. What did it speak to you?
     _____
     _____
     _____

   b. What do you want it to say to you?
     _____
     _____

6 | Why does God give us dreams and visions?
_____
_____
_____

a. If you don't completely understand them, is that okay?

_____

I believe our lack of understanding can serve as an inspiration to pursue Him for our answers.

7 | At the point when you ponder the imagery of the lioness, what would you like to learn?

_____

_____

_____

_____

_____

_____

> *"Vision looks inward and becomes duty. Vision looks outward and becomes aspiration. Vision looks upward and becomes faith."*[4]
>
> Stephen S. Wise

Rise Up Like a Lioness

I want you to drink a bit deeper of Numbers 23:19-23 (in my words) because if you are to awaken a lioness, these truths must surround your life:

Trust God, He does not lie or change His mind. When He speaks He acts and His promises endure. His blessing over your life cannot be reversed. He has not planned misfortune and trouble for you, but He will redeem it. He is with those who proclaim Him their king as He brings you forth in strength. Curses and magic cannot prevail against you. People will see His reflection in your life and declare His wonder.

This is the foundational promise on which we can rise up unafraid. If you know that God has gone before and behind you, why be afraid?

Looking for Affirmation

Even though I now declare this truth to you, when my "encounter" with the lioness happened I immediately reduced it by passing it through the grid of me. I looked at me and no longer saw her. Visions are given so that we lift our eyes and lose sight of the limitations of ourselves.

It is dangerous to ask someone to explain to you what they have not seen. I was responsible to interpret this vision in my life, but instead I put it before another.

8 | Have you ever taken your dreams, hopes, or God-directives to another, only to be discouraged?

_____

_____

_____

Do you understand that if you ask or involve the wrong people you will get the wrong input? It doesn't make them wrong; it means you were.

9 | Did you understand my reaction to my friend's assessment?

_____

_____

_____

No More Excuses

10 | Why did my friend's excusing me have the opposite effect on me?

_____

_____

_____

_____

11 | What have you been excused from participating in that God may even now be factoring you into?

_____

_____

_____

Are you ready to flip some excuses?

It's Not About You!

There is a big difference between awakening as a lioness and awakening a lioness. One is a collective expression; the other an individual attempt. Humans can collectively express things they never can portray individually. Just because I can sing does not make me the choir. A singer is not a choir, and a choir is not an individual singer but a collection of singers. I am God's daughter, but I am not the collective expression of the Bride of Christ.

How often have you thought of Jesus as a shepherd? Yet He is also a lamb. One is a human; the other an animal. Likewise, He is both a king and a lion. Here we explore the king, the bride, and the lioness.

Look...and Learn

A David-psalm...

> God's glory is on tour in the skies, God-craft on exhibit across the horizon. Madame Day holds classes every morning, Professor Night lectures each evening. Their words aren't heard, their voices aren't recorded, but their silence fills the earth: **unspoken truth is spoken everywhere.** God makes a huge dome for the sun—a superdome! The morning sun's a new husband leaping from his honeymoon bed, the daybreaking sun an athlete racing to the tape. That's how God's Word vaults across the skies from sunrise to sunset, melting ice, scorching deserts, warming hearts to faith. The revelation of God is whole and pulls our lives together. The signposts of God are clear and point out the right road. The life-maps of God are right, showing the way to joy. The directions of God are plain and easy on the eyes.
>
> Psalm 19:1-8

Creation is God's unspoken truth spoken everywhere!

Pride Play

Over the next week, be intentional to invite God into your dreams each night. Keep a journal next to you and record what happens.

Room for Reflection...

_____

_____

_____

_____

_____

_____

_____

_____

_____

_____

_____

_____

LIONESS LESSONS

▓ God wants you to have clarity of vision and the ability to write it down.

▓ Nature itself is a tool of vision. It is a constant expression of God's vision to see us free.

▓ Visions are given so that we lift our eyes and lose sight of the limitations of ourselves.

▓ There is a big difference between awakening as a lioness and awakening a lioness.

Pride Purpose
It's not about you!

FIERCE FACTS

- A lion's maximum speed: 30 miles per hour over 50 yards (48 kilometers per hour over 46 meters).[5]
- A lion's biggest jump: 12 feet (3.7 meters) vertical, 36 feet (10.8 meters) horizontal.[6]

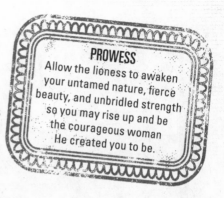

PROWESS

Allow the lioness to awaken your untamed nature, fierce beauty, and unbridled strength so you may rise up and be the courageous woman He created you to be.

Prayer Roar
I realize I have the potential to be a living, breathing solution to human problems. Lord, lead me as I embark on this journey!

(1) *E.L. Doctorow Quotes* (http://thinkexist.com/quotation/writing_is_an_exploration-you_start_from_nothing/204627.html, retrieved 11-28-2010). (2) *Napoleon Hill Quotes* (http://thinkexist.com/quotation/cherish_your_visions_and_your_dreams_as_they_are/14325.html, retrieved 11-28-2010). (3) *Helen Keller Quotes* (http://thinkexist.com/quotation/the_most_pathetic_person_in_the_world_is_someone/144261.html, retrieved 11-28-2010). (4) *Stephen S. Wise Quotes* (http://thinkexist.com/quotation/vision_looks_inward_and_becomes_duty-vision_looks/219992.html, retrieved 11-28-2010). (5) *Lion Facts* (http://www.lionlamb.us/lion/lionfact.html, retrieved 11-15-2010). (6) Ibid.

IMPRESSIONS

A FORCE UNSEEN 2

> *"If ever there comes a time when the women of the world*
> *come together purely and simply for the benefit of mankind,*
> *it will be a force such as the world has never known."*
>
> Matthew Arnold, 19th century British poet & philosopher

1 | What was *your* initial reaction to Matthew Arnold's quote that opened this chapter?

Overwhelmed	Awed	Challenged
Doubtful	Frightened	Inspired

Your own words _____

   a. How does this gathering of women differ from a gathering of feminists?

_____

_____

_____

_____

   b. In light of Arnold's statement, how does the following statement by Margaret Mead come into play?

_____

_____

"The solution to adult problems tomorrow depends on large measure upon how our children grow up today."[2]
Margaret Mead

2 | What do you think she is talking about?

_____

_____

_____

_____

_____

_____

...the truest answers are played out by how we choose to live. How we daily respond to life choices and opportunities will determine how we will be known in the history of our space in time.
[page 20]

a. Do you think we always have the future in mind as we go through the day to day?

_____

3 | What are some ways we can raise up or train our children in the following areas to position them as future solutions for the potential problems of tomorrow?

As a group, discuss some strategies or ideas to address the following:

Gender Prejudice (prejudices can go both ways):

_____

_____

Materialism & Greed:

_____

_____

Honor & Respect:

_____

_____

Marriage & Family:

_____

_____

Sexual Ethics, Purity & Virtue:

_____

_____

We live in a world filled with ever-increasing opportunities. We are not limited like our sisters of the 1800s. We have the ability to stretch forth and reach out to others to do this well. We must look back *and* ahead.

At Ease with Strength, At Rest with Power

4 | Not only are our lives and talents an entrustment, but the very timing of our days is one as well. How does the scripture on the right weigh in on this?

_____

_____

_____

_____

_____

_____

_____

_____

_____

When someone has been given much, much will be required in return; and when someone has been entrusted with much, even more will be required.

Luke 12:48 NLT

Great gifts mean great responsibilities; greater gifts, greater responsibilities!

Luke 12:48

In addition to the definition given on page 21 of the book, "stretch" or "to stretch" can mean: to make bigger, enlarge, widen, draw out, reach out, extend, elasticity, expand, yield, flexible, unfold, unroll, and straighten.[3]

5 | What are some of the areas in your life that need to be stretched?

_____

_____

_____

_____

a. What are some areas that have already been stretched? (You will have at least *figurative* stretch marks to prove it.)

_____

_____

_____

b. How does the lioness *initially* stretch your perception of yourself?

_____

_____

_____

6 | "To stretch" is very different than "to strive." Striving is awkward, uncomfortable, and unattractive.

a. Is there an area in your life in which you are presently striving? (To honestly answer this, think of areas that feel forced.)

_____

_____

7 | Statues and revelations both have the power to awe and inspire.

a. What is the most inspiring statue you have seen?

_____

b. What did it inspire in you?

_____

_____

c. What is the difference between a statue and a revelation?

_____

_____

_____

8 | If it is true that we become what we behold, how important is the following?

Our view of ourselves:

_____

_____

The imagery and images that we allow entrance into our lives:

_____

_____

9 | What did the concept of *"at ease with strength and rest with power"* impress upon you?

_____

_____

_____

_____

When I read this description of the women God is empowering, I think of gracious or graceful women. Grace enables us to be gracious, kind, and generous to others. When we strive, we are usually restless, ungracious, stingy, and unkind.

Your salvation requires you to turn back to me and stop your silly efforts to save yourselves. Your strength will come from settling down in complete dependence on me—The very thing you've been unwilling to do.

Isaiah 30:15

> *We live and move in him, can't get away from him! One of your poets said it well: "We're the God-created."*
>
> Acts 17:28

It is ridiculous to imagine we can save our-selves! Strength comes from rest, and depen-dence produces ease. Remember, it is in him that we live, move, and have our being.

To echo the wisdom of *The Lion King*, "He lives in you. Because he lives in us, we are alive in Him."

10 | True strength from God involves relinquish-ing control. In the eyes of most, this pros-pect is terrifying. But the truth is that we are no more in control than we can save ourselves; so much in life is beyond our control. Freedom is found in surrendering control to Him.

a. Do you know women who are afraid of their strength?

_____

b. Are you?

_____

c. Why do you think this is?

_____

11 | Could it be that acknowledging strength makes you responsible?

_____

Virtuous and Capable

> *Who can find a virtuous and capable wife? She is more precious than rubies. Her husband can trust her, and she will greatly enrich his life. She brings him good, not harm, all the days of her life.*
>
> Proverbs 31:10-12 NLT

I fear there is so much more here than we've yet to express in and through our lives. First, my experience is that we have virtuous women in the Church and capable women outside the Church. We need to give expression to both. Church is not a place we go or an event we attend; you and I are the Church.

In this merger of virtue and talent, there's a recipe of sorts:

◆ To virtue, purity, and moral fortitude, add capabilities.
◆ To these capabilities, talents, or giftings, add increasing measures of purity and virtue.
◆ Combine it all by gently stirring.
◆ Then, increase the speed on the blending process until you are beating the combination on high and the batter is uniform in consistency.
◆ Pour the batter into a cake pan and place it in the oven for an hour.
◆ When it springs back into shape at your touch, God's refining is complete and the cake is ready to be served to others.

If we allow God's refining process to have its way, it will produce what is precious. The precious comes from mining and refining. Proverbs 31 goes on to say this woman is trustworthy. To be trustworthy one must be faithful, and the faithful always multiply what is in their care. Therefore, this is the progression here as well. Virtuous and capable women enrich the lives of others. The revelation of a lioness will not or should not diminish your husband, family, community, or church; it should enrich them!

And lastly, the virtuous, capable, precious, and trustworthy who enrich the lives of others bring good and not harm. We bring out the best as well as bring our best to others. It is the ability to lend strength and empower. Conversely, *harm* damages, spoils, and impairs the potential of others. Harm puts others at risk. "Good" is not a concept; it is something we do.

> *"It is not enough to outline gigantic programs on paper.*
> *I must write my ideas on the earth."*[4]
>
> Emile Pereire

12 | Ultimately, we must live out God's ideas so they might be revealed on earth. What God-ideas does your life presently display?

_____

_____

_____

_____

13 | Let's return to the concept of this force unseen by exploring Alexander the Great's insight:

"I am not afraid of an army of lions led by a sheep;
I am afraid of an army of sheep led by a lion."[5]

a. For me, this was again another breath-taking quote. Can you imagine the power of the Church positioned like this? We are a host of sheep. Our Lion Lord is the Captain of the host. Is this how we currently look? Or are we more like an army of lions raging against the leadership of sheep?

_____

_____

b. In the two columns, list some attributes that come to mind when you contrast sheep with lions.

Sheep	Lions

This isn't the first time we have been presented with this range of creature concepts. Check out the instructions of Jesus below:

Look, I am sending you out as sheep among wolves.
So be as shrewd as snakes and harmless as doves.

Matthew 10:16 NLT

The Message elaborates further:

Stay alert. This is hazardous work I'm assigning you. You're going to
be like sheep running through a wolf pack, so don't call attention
to yourselves. Be as cunning as a snake, inoffensive as a dove.

Matthew 10:16

In the scripture reference above, the dove is described as *harmless* and *inoffensive*. To be *harmless* means your presence poses no threat. It means we are to be safe, risk-free, undamaging, not dangerous, nontoxic, undisruptive, and non-detrimental.[6] *Inoffensive* is additionally defined as innocent, innocuous, mild, and unobjectionable.[7]

Isn't it interesting that these are already some of the concepts introduced for the Proverbs 31 woman?

14 | Moving on to the end of the spectrum, the snake is described as "shrewd and cunning." To be *shrewd* is to be astute, sharp, on the ball, smart, perceptive, insightful, and wise.[8] *Cunning* can be defined as clever, inventive, resourceful, ingenious, skilled, creative, and having expertise.[9] After reading the list, you can see that none of these attributes are wicked. It is just that serpents use these skills for the wrong end.

What are some areas in which you need to be harmless and less offensive? (List at least 2.)

_____

_____

What are some areas in which you need to add in shrewd and crafty? (List at least 2.)

_____

_____

There is a lot of room for movement, learning, and strategy in the comparison of these vastly different creatures. Again, remember this is the very reason God uses birds and beasts to teach us wisdom.

Wind Words

15 | What does the question "Are your ears awake?" mean to you?

_____

_____

_____

a. Has there been a time when you, like me, have found yourself too familiar with God's Word?

_____

_____

_____

b. What do you do to fight the complacency of familiarity?

_____

_____

_____

_____

c. Has the addition of The Message paraphrase helped you to hear your usual version of the Bible with more awe?

_____

It is interesting that the following is the introduction for our virtuous and capable Proverbs 31 woman:

> *Speak up for the people who have no voice, for the rights of all the down-and-outers. Speak out for justice! Stand up for the poor and destitute!*
>
> Proverbs 31:8-9

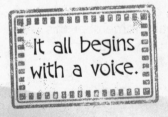

It all begins with a voice.

Things change when we speak up on behalf of others who have been silenced. Injustice trembles when we stand up for the rights of others rather than fighting solely for our own. When we cheer on justice and champion its cause, darkness trembles and hope returns to the formerly hopeless. When we rise from our complacency for the sake of the poor and destitute, they have a presence in the courts of life.

⊠ HUNT QUEST ⊠

Recently I read an article. In it, Archbishop Desmond Tutu was asked by Oprah what he would recommend for the world in order to experience real world peace. He answered:

"I want to suggest that women start a revolution."[10]

Okay...wow. Let it begin here and now.

To locate areas of need in your immediate community:
+ Read your local newspaper.
+ Call a foster child agency.
+ Call a community center.
+ Contact your police department.

Where is the greatest need? Perhaps all it will take to answer the following questions is you opening your eyes and ears to see and hear what you previously missed amid all the noise.

+ Who in your immediate world needs your voice?

_____

_____

+ Who are the down and out who need you to lift them?

_____

_____

+ Who needs your voice so they might have justice?

_____

_____

+ Strategize as a group how you can get involved...

_____

_____

Perhaps there are already amazing organizations and churches praying for your support, talents, prayer, generosity, and partnership. I know I'd love to see you on board with some of the outreaches we're involved with because we can't do what we do without you. But, what is God telling you to do?

_____

_____

_____

_____

You can see, my lovely, virtuous, capable, inoffensive, cunning, harmless, shrewd, trustworthy, faithful lionesses who enrich the lives of those around you and gather to create strategy on how to "do good"—we have a big challenge before us!

Pride Play

Bring a publication with you to your next gathering.

How does that newspaper, magazine, or article speak of this moment in history?

_____

_____

As a group, discuss the common threads between your articles.

_____

_____

_____

_____

What is it that our world is crying out for?

_____

_____

_____

How can your virtue and capabilities help bring solution?

_____

_____

_____

LIONESS LESSONS

- ✖ Striving is unattractive, but stretching is invaluable; it extends your reach and prevents injury.

- ✖ We have a lot to learn from snakes and doves.

- ✖ Everything begins with a voice.

Pride Purpose

You, lovely one, have the potential to be a living, breathing solution to human problems. You are invited to be part of the company of the virtuous and capable!

PROWESS
Like the lioness, learn to be at ease with your strength and at rest with your power.

FIERCE FACTS

- Lions can hear a prey from a distance of one mile.[11]
- The sense of smell of a lion is so sharp that it cannot only tell if prey is nearby, but also ascertain how long ago it was in the area.[12]

Prayer Roar

I am ready to give expression to lovely, virtuous, capable, inoffensive, cunning, harmless, shrewd, trustworthy, faithful lioness daughters who enrich the lives of those around me and gather to strategize how to "do good." I am willing to take on this challenge!

(1) Lisa Bevere, *Lioness Arising* (Colorado Springs, CO: Waterbrook Press, 2010) p. 19. (2) *Margaret Mead Quotes* (http://thinkexist.com/quotation/the_solution_to_adult_problems_tomorrow_depends/216325.html, retrieved 11-22-2010). (3) *MSN Encarta Dictionary & Thesaurus* (http://encarta.msn.com, retrieved 11-22-2010). (4) See note 1., p. 25. (5) *Alexander the Great Quotes* (http://www.brainyquote.com/quotes/authors/a/alexander_the_great.html, retrieved 11-22-2010). (6) See note 3. (7) Ibid. (8) Ibid. (9) Ibid. (10) The Oprah Magazine: *O's Guide to Life* (Birmingham, AL: Hearst Communications, Inc., 2007), p. 287. (11) *Facts about Lion* (http://lifestyle.iloveindia.com/lounge/facts-about-lion-1509.html, retrieved 11-11-2010). (12) Ibid.

IMPRESSIONS

DANGEROUSLY AWAKE 3

1 | To begin, let's return to the story of the collared lion, his protective lioness, and the ranger's comment, "To get to *him* we will have to tranquilize *her*."

a. How did the story of the collared lion and his lioness make you feel as a woman?

_____

_____

_____

_____

b. What parallels can you see between this interaction and how our enemy operates?

_____

_____

_____

_____

c. Do you think the enemy frequently uses this tactic?

_____

_____

d. Who is at risk if *you* are tranquilized?

_____

_____

As the woman is described as a guardian of the heart in Proverbs 31, it would make sense that she can have the capacity to create or deny access to the man. Eve's actions alone proved this theory true.

2 | How did the concepts of "dangerous" and "fully awake" strike you? Did you feel it stir something within?

_____

_____

_____

_____

Sedated by the Day to Day

I find it intriguing that I closed the *Nurture* book with the following verses from Romans 13 yet felt compelled to open this book with its charge. I know of no better passage than the following to illustrate what it means to be dangerous and fully awake. In this study we are going to break it down a bit further.

> *But make sure that you don't get so **absorbed and exhausted** in taking care of all your day-by-day obligations... (verse 11)*

First, we are warned against being *absorbed and exhausted* by our day-to-day obligations. In this context, *absorb* means: to soak up, take in, suck up, and engrossed.[1]

Most of us know at least how exhaustion feels, but let's investigate what *exhausted* means. It is: the state of being worn out, beat, drained, bushed, depleted, fatigued, weakened, used up, consumed, and finished. The opposite of *exhausted* is "renewed" and "refreshed," and the opposite of *absorbed* is "to exude" and "radiate."[2]

Those who wait upon the Lord find their strength renewed, their lives refreshed, and they exude His radiance. Conversely, the day to day will suck the life out of you until you are depleted with nothing left to give. This exhausted, absorbed state means you run the risk...

> *that you lose track of the time and doze off, oblivious to God. (verse 11)*

When we're exhausted, it's easy to lose track of time. I imagine I've been asleep five minutes when it's actually been half an hour. A late start can begin your whole day off course. You see, time travels a path. Each day of our lives is a course or journey of 24 hours. But when you're exhausted, you risk wandering off course. You are more aware of your *state of exhaustion* than you are of the *path of God*. To be oblivious to God means to be unaware, ignorant, and insensible of His presence, directives, and purpose. The next verse serves to give a sense of timing to all who might have lost their perspective:

The night is about over, dawn is about to break. (verse 12)

They say it's darkest before dawn. If this is true of the shifting from night to day in our present season, then it is understandable why it is easy to miss what is coming. To prevent this, we are charged to:

Be up and awake to what God is doing! (verse 12)

Again, I love the simplicity of this. We don't have to be up running around, figuring out what we are doing. We don't have to figure out what everyone else is or is not doing. We are to rise up and take note of what *He* (God) is doing! It is only when we perceive what He is doing that we truly discover what we are called to do.

God is putting the finishing touches on the salvation work he began when we first believed. (verse 12)

His work is almost complete, and because of this...

We can't afford to waste a minute, must not squander these precious daylight hours in frivolity and indulgence, in sleeping around and dissipation, in bickering and grabbing everything in sight. (verse 13)

Here, Paul is no longer tracking time by days; he has switched to measuring time in the increments of hours and minutes. We are charged not to waste a minute or squander an hour.

Get out of bed and get dressed! Don't loiter and linger, waiting until the very last minute. Dress yourselves in Christ, and be up and about! (verse 14)

Okay, this is not complicated. Find your feet, get in motion, and put on your clothes. But we are entrusted with garments that we cannot purchase; we are to clothe ourselves in Him.

Jesus told His parents He had to be about His Father's business. It is time we did the same.

Reviewing this collection of verses in its entirety makes me think there is a progressive relation between exhaustion and squandered time. It is easy to see how the two could combine and create a vicious cycle of distraction, disregard, and dissipation.

3 | Define the following symptoms of *oblivious, absorbed exhaustion*:

Frivolity: _____

Indulgence: _____

Sleeping around: _____

Dissipation: _____

Bickering: _____

Grabbing everything in sight: _____

    a. Do you see these symptoms of a sleepy bride present in the Church today?

    _____

Answers, Not Problems

4 | Since we've declared you an answer, let's measure your involvement with problems:

On a scale of 1 to 5 (1 being lowest, 5 being highest), answer the following questions:

I feel valued by leadership in my workplace. _____
I am a leader in my workplace. _____

I feel valued by the leadership in my church. _____
I am a leader in my church. _____
My input and contribution is encouraged in my workplace. _____
There is opportunity for advancement in my workplace. _____
My input and contribution is encouraged in my church. _____
There is opportunity for advancement in my church. _____
My husband values my input. _____
My children value my input. _____
I value the input of other women. _____

Rage and judgment will always make problems the focus and punishment the goal. We need to allow love and the righteous anger that seeks restoration to guide our actions.

⊠ HUNT QUEST ⊠

There is a problem out there that God created you to answer. To locate it, use some of the following questions and jot down the answers that apply:

Look around your workplace, school, or church and notice someone who needs a friend. Who in your world of influence have you noticed is troubled?

_____

How could you encourage or comfort them?

_____

_____

What are you good at? (This could be anything from a hobby to making people laugh.)

_____

_____

What do you love doing?

_____

_____

Are you a teacher? mother? doctor? actress? political or church leader? author or artist? friend? networker? organizer? lawyer or lobbyist? Given your area of work or expertise, what is in your power to solve?

_____

_____

_____

_____

Sleeveless in Sodom

Ask any group of Christians what the sins of Sodom and Gomorrah were, and you are sure to get a list that contains the following: homosexuality, sexual sin, idolatry, greed, wickedness, and godlessness. No doubt they were guilty of all of the above, *but* this was not the root of Sodom's sin issues. The prophet Ezekiel exposes it as follows:

> *Now this was the sin of your sister Sodom: She and her daughters were **arrogant, overfed and unconcerned;** they did not help the poor and needy. They were haughty and did detestable things before me. Therefore I did away with them as you have seen.*
>
> Ezekiel 16:49-50 NIV

The Message describes it this way:

> *The sin of your sister Sodom was this: She lived with her daughters in the **lap of luxury**—proud, gluttonous, and lazy. They ignored the oppressed and the poor. They put on airs and lived obscene lives. And you know what happened: I did away with them.*

Yes, Sodom sinned in all the manners listed above, but it would appear the root cause of her many sins was found in her threefold heart condition of arrogance, overindulgence, and lazy apathy. This detached, superior attitude caused her to ignore the oppressed, in need, and poor in her midst. So rather than pouncing on homosexuality as Sodom's ultimate and root sin, perhaps we should ask ourselves the question that may hit closer to home: Are we proud, overfed, and unconcerned?

5 | List areas where you may be:

Overfed	Unconcerned
i.e. TV	i.e. my neighbors

We also tend to hold up the people of Sodom as though they were the worst of the worst, but hear what God says when He compared them to His people:

> *You have done far more detestable things than your sisters ever did. They seem righteous compared to you. Shame on you! Your sins are so terrible that you make your sisters seem righteous, even virtuous. ... In your proud days you held Sodom in contempt.*
>
> Ezekiel 16:51-52, 56 NLT

I am ready for an end of the reign of pride. I want it exposed in my life so I can truly see my condition and the condition of those around me.

The root of Sodom's sin was an arrogant, self-indulgent, lazy, gluttonous lifestyle that had a blatant disregard for the poor in their midst. The NKJV says they had "abundance of idleness," and they did not "strengthen the hands of the poor."

So much for Sodom; now let's move on to "sleeveless."

The byproduct of exhaustion, overindulgence, and apathy is a glaring lack of purpose. One of the symptoms of this as individuals—and corporately as the church—is being distracted or fixated on the small and insignificant while missing the large and significant. This is nothing new.

> *Blind guides! You strain your water so you won't accidentally swallow a gnat, but you swallow a camel!*
>
> Matthew 23:24 NLT

There is great risk when our guides are blind.

Recently I posted a question to Twitter, which then posted to my Facebook account. I asked whether or not it was appropriate for a female minister to speak sleeveless.

First, allow me to be clear: *I wanted* the opinions of others. What caught me off guard was how many and how intense the varying answers became.

Mixed into the 450 plus responses was an intense battle. It seemed those who were of the opinion that sleeveless is fine and those who felt it is not had a holy jihad of sorts on my Facebook page while I was recording the *Lioness Arising* audio book in Focus on the Family's studio. Talk about passion! It got out of hand, and I had to delete the strand of comments.

In contrast, I had earlier posted this alarming statistic on "gendercide" (the killing of people based on gender): **50 million women are missing from the earth due to gendercide, and each year another 2 million go missing.**[3]

There were perhaps 40 responses from the 35,000 people whom I have access to on Facebook; that is barely a blip on the radar screen. Yet, the sleeveless question elicited nearly 500. I was countered with the insight, "A question always invites more response than a statement." True. But as I cited in *Lioness Arising*, I had made a comment about women leading that had likewise elicited such a massive response. This too caused an uproar.

So, my question becomes: *Are we more comfortable with women dying than we are with them leading?*

Two million women dead or missing is a camel! Sleeveless is a gnat.

6 | What are some major areas in your life you may be neglecting by arguing about minor areas?

Camels   Gnats

_____   _____

_____   _____

_____   _____

7 | How does the story of Jonah fit into this?

_____

_____

_____

a. What was Jonah's gnat?

_____

b. What was his camel?

_____

c. How do anger and judgment cause our focus to be skewed?

_____

_____

_____

_____

> *"When we look squarely at injustice and get involved, we actually feel less pain, not more, because we overcome the gnawing guilt and despair that festers under our numbness. We clean the wound—our own and others'—and it can finally heal."*[4]
>
> Archbishop Desmond Tutu

Your Unique Expression

8 | How would you like to define the expression of a fierce, wild lioness of a Christian woman?

From the list below, choose the words that resonate with you. Feel free to write in your own as well.

Graceful	Tender	Fierce	Fearless
Stunning	Golden	Nurturing	Hunter
Might	Confident	Bold	Protective

Ferocious	Majestic	Awake	At ease
Strength	Beautiful	Team	Passionate
Dangerous	Prophetic	Wild	

Your own words _____

Wake-up Duty

9 | What did the story of my sorority wake-up duty speak to you?

_____
_____
_____

a. How do you respond when awakened?

_____
_____

b. Do you think the Church may be talking in her sleep?

_____

c. Do you believe that when people are truly awake or quickened to God and aware of what He is doing that they are positioned to realize what they are called to be a part of?

_____

Legend Lioness

"I do not believe in using women in combat, because females are too fierce."[5]

Margaret Mead

Awaken Something Fierce

Do not imagine that just because a lioness is female she is not a lion. The term *lion* captures both male and female of the species, just as *human* includes both genders.

10 | Most of us know what "nurture" looks like, but what do we know of "fierce"?

_____
_____

a. Do you believe fierce can produce focus?

_____

11 | What was your reaction the first time you heard of a cruel atrocity such as rape, sex trafficking, or murder?

_____

_____

_____

_____

Were you outraged? The young and awake...*respond.*

a. If you are a mother, have you ever envisioned how you would respond to someone kidnapping or hurting your child?

_____

b. If you are not a mother, can you imagine how you would respond to someone hurting your younger brother or sister?

_____

_____

_____

c. What was your response? Was it passive, or was it more like something out of Hosea?

_____

_____

_____

So now I will attack you like a lion, like a leopard that lurks along the road. Like a bear whose cubs have been taken away, I will tear out your heart. I will devour you like a hungry lioness and mangle you like a wild animal.

Hosea 13:7-8 NLT

d. Did you know this is a natural, possibly God-breathed response? (Not the killing and eating part, but the fierce.)

_____

12 | How does "awake" differ from sad or upset?

_____
_____
_____
_____

a. Can you be upset and asleep?

_____

b. What provokes a fierce response in you that even now requires prayer?

_____
_____
_____
_____

Legend Lioness

"There will never be complete equality until women themselves help to make laws and elect lawmakers."[6]

Susan B. Anthony, campaigned for the vote for U.S. women

God Did Not Save You to Tame You

God does not reveal Himself as limitless and infinite in order to limit us. He does it to impart the realization of the vastness of who He is, while at once reminding us we are in Him.

13 | What is the difference between being a Christian and merely acting like one?

_____
_____
_____
_____

a. What does the word "Christian" mean?

_____

_____

_____

> *God's Spirit is on me; he's chosen me to preach the Message*
> *of good news to the poor, sent me to announce pardon to prisoners*
> *and recovery of sight to the blind, to set the burdened and*
> *battered free, to announce, "This is God's year to act!"*
>
> Luke 4:18-19

14 | List 4 things God's Spirit empowers us to do.

1. _____

2. _____

3. _____

4. _____

The following verses in Luke 4 read as follows:

> *He rolled up the scroll, handed it back to the assistant, and sat down.*
> *Every eye in the place was on him, intent. Then he started in, "You've just*
> *heard Scripture make history. It came true just now in this place."*
>
> Luke 4:20-21

I want the scriptures to make history in my life. I believe it is our destiny. But as you and I already know:

> *"Well-behaved women rarely make history."[7]*
>
> Laurel Thatcher Ulrich

15 | Are you willing and ready to run the risk of appearing ill-behaved?

_____

16 | List at least one woman not mentioned in the book who was questioned in her immediate time period but later on noted as a history maker.

_____

17 | What is your greatest area of concern?

_____

_____

a. Can you behave the same and see it change?

_____

b. What is in your power to fiercely defend?

_____

_____

_____

Pride Play

Watch a lion/lioness documentary on YouTube or rent one from your local library. Study the ways of the lioness and see what God reveals to your pride!

Room for Reflection...

_____

_____

_____

_____

_____

_____

_____

_____

LIONESS LESSONS

- ✖ To get to the men, the enemy tranquilizes the women.

- ✖ The fully awake…respond.

- ✖ There is a problem out there that God created you to answer.

- ✖ The root of Sodom's sin was arrogance and being overfed and unconcerned.

- ✖ It is better to swallow a gnat than a camel.

- ✖ The well-behaved rarely make history.

Pride Purpose

There is nothing more dangerous than being on your feet and fully awake.

PROWESS
God did not save you to tame you.

FIERCE FACTS

- The largest lion recorded to date was almost 11 feet long and weighed nearly 700 pounds.[10]
- The eyesight of a lion is five times better than that of a human.[11]

Prayer Roar

I am ready to be dangerous and fully awake. I refuse to be absorbed by my day to day, fall asleep, and miss out on what God is doing. I will not be tranquilized; I will respond. Expose the areas in my life where I am overfed and unconcerned. Forgive me for swallowing camels. I am ready to be a history-making woman.

(1) *MSN Encarta Dictionary & Thesaurus* (http://encarta.msn.com, retrieved 11-22-2010). (2) Ibid. (3) Nicholas D. Kristof and Sheryl WuDunn, *Half the Sky: Turning Oppression into Opportunity for Women Worldwide* (New York: Knopf, 2009), xviii. (4) Archbishop Desmond Tutu, *Believe* (Boulder, CO: Blue Mountain Press, 2007), p. 68. (5) *Margaret Mead Quotes* (http://www.brainyquote. com/quotes/authors/m/margaret_mead.html, retrieved 11-16-2010). (6) *Women Who Changed the World: Fifty Inspirational Women Who Shaped History* (Millers Point NSW, Australia: Pier 9, 2006), p. 66. (7) *Laurel Thatcher Ulrich Quotes* (http://thinkexist.com/quotation/well-behaved_ women_rarely_make/180481.html, retrieved 11-22-2010). (8) See note 6., p. 134. (9) Ibid., p. 90. (10) *Facts about Lion* (http://lifestyle.iloveindia.com/lounge/facts-about-lion-1509.html, retrieved 11-11-2010). (11) Ibid.

IMPRESSIONS

THE SUM OF FEAR AND WONDER **4**

Then our lioness sighs contently as she sums up her beauty:
"I am fearfully and wonderfully made."
[page 58]

1 | What did the story of the lioness as the sum of fear and wonder speak to you?

_____

_____

_____

a. Is it easy for you to see the lioness as fearfully and wonderfully made? Why?

_____

_____

_____

b. Is it hard for you to see yourself as marvelous and fearfully wonderful? Why?

_____

_____

_____

2 | If you have given birth to a child, how did you feel afterward—other than exhausted?

_____

   a. How did you see your body after that experience?

_____

_____

It wasn't until my second childbirth that I realized my body was capable of more than I had experienced before.

The lioness knows that her beauty is revealed in her strength. As lovely as she is, the lioness knows her wonder is expressed in what she can actually *do* more than in how she *looks*.

3 | List three wonderful things you, or your body, can do.

   1. _____

   2. _____

   3. _____

4 | God says you are a work of His wonder. What strength, or area of strength, will you now call "beautiful"?

_____

_____

Her attractiveness is undeniable because her power is unquestionable. The lioness knows what she is capable of and revels in the wonder of it. She rejoices in this capacity, bringing glory to her Creator.

You are a daughter of the Most High, and His beauty and power are beyond description and above question. Denying and diminishing this assignment of God's love, beauty, and wonder is not modesty; it is a slap in His face. Look again at Psalm 139 from The Message:

Oh yes, you shaped me first inside, then out; you formed me in my mother's womb. I thank you, High God—you're breathtaking! Body and soul, I am marvelously made! I worship in adoration—what a creation!

You know me inside and out, you know every bone in my body; you know exactly how I was made, bit by bit, how I was sculpted from nothing into something. . . . Oh, let me rise in the morning and live always with you!

(verses 13-15, 18)

David's words capture what the Bride's response should sound like. We are to be so awed by the handiwork of God in our individual bodies—how they were formed first inside, then out—that we declare God breathtaking! When we look at the hands and feet, and the marvel of the unseen working of the human body, we should worship God in adoration at the wonder of us.

I know I am challenging you here, but you—all of you—inspire awe. Let's stop denying the miracle of God in us. This isn't an issue of vanity but of honoring God as our Creator.

5 | How does this fly in the face of a culture that measures people based on how they look (models) or pretend (actors), rather than by their contribution?

_____

_____

_____

   a. Does fashion truly strengthen others?

_____

   b. Are photos an accurate assessment of beauty?

_____

We live in a day when people are roaming the earth afraid and wondering what is going on. Could it be we are distracted by pretenses and false images?

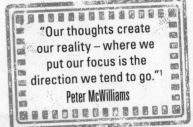

"Our thoughts create our reality – where we put our focus is the direction we tend to go."[1]
Peter McWilliams

Let's make the shift. It is time we displayed God's fearsome wonder in and through our lives.

Let's celebrate all the potential He has hidden within us by becoming the strongest women we can be—spirit, soul, and body!

Mistaken for Buff, and Skinny Fat

I really think I wanted to look like the original Sarah Connor because deep down I wanted to be an action hero. We all want to find out that we are stronger than we ever imagined. I also think we want to know that seasons of hardship have the power to transform us.

Perhaps you are in the midst of a hardship that could potentially transform you. Maybe this is a season of personal training so you will be strong at the time of your release.

6 | Have any of you had a physical assessment that went as poorly as mine?

_____

Is there anyone else out there who was silly enough to think she was strong, or worse yet, buff, just because she looked good in her clothes?

a. Why are periodic life assessments of all sorts valuable? (Medical and dental exams, challenging relational conflicts, Bible studies, etc.)

_____

_____

Your weight is NOT the most accurate reflection of what you are made of! It is a number. Your composition and muscle mass are indicators of your potential strength. But for any muscle to have strength, it must be developed through use. I think it's profound that to build muscle you must lift weights or bear a load.

Our culture awards many just because they "look good," but God is inviting us higher.

7 | I believe you are in this study because it is more important to you to "do good" rather than merely "look good." So, what must happen if we are to actually have the strength to "do good"?

_____

—————————————
—————————————
—————————————

A People Invincible

On your feet, Daughter of Zion!
Be threshed of chaff, be refined of dross.
I'm remaking you into a people invincible.

Micah 4:13

8 | I love that the first thing God says is, *"Find your feet, girl. Arise!"* This verse describes the makeover process. List some components you see:

—————————————
—————————————

a. Do you think our focus has been more on being invisible, or, to be more accurate, in the hope of disappearing or escaping hardship?

—————————————
—————————————

b. How often do we (or the media) associate God's people with the invincible?

—————————————
—————————————
—————————————

c. When did you last feel invincible? Why?

—————————————
—————————————

(If you are having a difficult time remembering when you last felt invincible, usually this exhilaration happens immediately after you conquer a fear or overcome a hardship.)

*God will give you new life again. He'll redeem you from your enemies. But for right now, they're ganged up against you, many godless peoples, saying, "Kick her when she's down! Violate her! We want to see Zion grovel in the dirt." These blasphemers have no idea what God is thinking and doing in this. They don't know that this is the making of God's people, that they are **wheat being threshed, gold being refined.***

Micah 4:10-12

9 | Threshing happens through the process of sifting and shaking. Gold is refined by exposure to intense heat.

Describe the last time you felt sifted and shaken:

_____

_____

_____

Describe the last time you felt refined by fire:

_____

_____

_____

a. What was the last hardship you went through? What did it produce in your life?

_____

_____

_____

_____

10 | Do you think there is some truth in the way the world sees us or the criticisms they make? If so, why?

_____

_____

_____

There are times it is best to humble ourselves and agree with those who attack us. Jesus outlined this in the following verse:

When you are on the way to court with your adversary, settle your differences quickly. Otherwise, your accuser may hand you over to the judge, who will hand you over to an officer, and you will be thrown into prison.

Matthew 5:25 NLT

*Or say you're out on the street and an old enemy accosts you. Don't lose a minute. Make the first move; **make things right with him.** After all, if you leave the first move to him, knowing his track record, you're likely to end up in court, maybe even jail.*

Matthew 5:25

11 | When was the last time you did this? What was the result?

_____

_____

_____

And they overcame him by the blood of the Lamb and by the word of their testimony, and they did not love their lives to the death.

Revelation 12:11 NKJV

12 | This scripture from the book of Revelation is definitely one of heavy weight. Why do you think that frequently when it is quoted, the third point ("they did not love their lives to the death") is left off?

_____

_____

_____

The blood is what He shed, the testimony is what He has done in us, and loving not our lives even unto death is the cross. The cross does not invite us to be busy; it invites us to lay down our lives and pick up His. Taking up the cross, following Him, and denying ourselves are all weight-bearing, strength-building Christian life exercises.

Betrayed by Busy

Checkups or assessments are necessary, but that doesn't mean they are always painless or fun. Now it is time to move out of the gym and visit the Trainer or Doctor—Jesus. Let's process the assessment of the churches in the book of Revelation a bit closer:

> *I see right through your work. You have a reputation for vigor and zest, but you're dead, stone-dead. **Up on your feet!** Take a deep breath! Maybe there's life in you yet. But I wouldn't know it by looking at **your busywork; nothing of God's work** has been completed. Your condition is desperate. Think of the gift you once had in your hands, the Message you heard with your ears—grasp it again and turn back to God. **If you pull the covers back over your head and sleep on,** oblivious to God, I'll return when you least expect it, break into your life like a thief in the night.*

Revelation 3:1-3

We don't want a work that is dead and see-through. Let's build that which is strong and substantive. We see this theme repeated over and over again: Find your feet, stop striving in your busyness, and wake up!

To be clear, there is a big difference between being busy and being effective. I know I can be busy all day yet get nothing truly done. Like Mary we must choose to invest in what can't be taken from us. Sitting at His feet builds a strength that slinging pots and pans cannot. To bring this in balance, "busy" doesn't always equal "ineffective." There is a vast difference between busywork, busy bodies, and a full life.

◼ HUNT QUEST ◼

13 | On the scale, rate your normal day:

Busy--Effective

Some of us (notice I am included here) are ineffective because we take on too much.

a. List the things that you know are God's work for you right now. (I.e. husband, children, school, home, job, etc.)

_____

_____

_____

_____

b. What things interrupt these and distract you with "busy"? (I.e. drama, cell phone, Facebook, Internet, Home Shopping Network, projects you're involved with, TV, etc.)

_____

_____

_____

_____

_____

_____

c. What can be reduced, reprioritized, or eliminated?

_____

_____

_____

_____

Legend Lioness

"Look at a day when you are supremely satisfied at the end. It's not a day when you lounge around doing nothing; it's when you've had everything to do, and you've done it."[3]

Margaret Thatcher

The last church was corrected for being too busy with the non-essentials. The next church we will visit is corrected for not knowing their true condition.

I know you inside and out, and find little to my liking. You're not cold, you're not hot—far better to be either cold or hot! You're stale. You're stagnant. You make me want to vomit. You brag, "I'm rich, I've got it made, I need nothing from anyone," oblivious that in fact you're a pitiful, blind beggar, threadbare and homeless.

Here's what I want you to do: Buy your gold from me, gold that's been through the refiner's fire. Then you'll be rich. Buy your clothes from me, clothes designed in Heaven. You've gone around half-naked long enough. And buy medicine for your eyes from me so you can see, really see.

Revelation 3:15-18

14 | Referring to the scripture above, what are some ways the modern Church says: "I'm rich, I've got it made, I need nothing from anyone"?

_____

_____

_____

_____

a. What are some of the ways we, as individuals, say this?

_____

_____

b. How do we say it without words?

_____

_____

Jesus saw through the works of the last church; with this one He sees through them! I wouldn't like Jesus to say, "I know you completely and find little to My liking!" Isn't it better to hear it now when adjustments can be made?

It seems they lacked passion.
An indifferent church is a deceived church.
A church that brags about its wealth is destitute.
We are blessed to be a blessing, not to isolate and insulate ourselves from the needs of others.

To correct their wretched condition, Jesus counsels them to begin shopping with Him. First, He recommends they buy gold that's been refined. This is the very gold we discussed earlier that comes through obedience during hardship and suffering, and it alone brings true riches.

Next, Jesus admonishes a change of wardrobe. He suggests they purchase clothing from Him. We obviously cannot attempt a monetary exchange with heaven to buy clothing, but there does seem to be a currency we can lift heavenward.

Second Corinthians 5 talks about our longing to be clothed with the incorruptible. Our prayers and the acknowledgment of the current, awkward fit of our present apparel set the fashioning of our heavenly designs into motion.

And lastly, we buy with our prayers the medicine our eyes need that we might truly see. Jesus is the Great Physician, and the prescription that restores sight will look different for each of us.

Deception about our true condition puts us at risk. We are easily tricked into trusting in fool's gold rather than incorruptible riches. It leaves us half-naked, homeless, and blind.

15 | Do you think Jesus is harsh in the passage from Revelation 3? If so, why do you think there is such intensity and passion in His voice?

_____

_____

_____

The people I love, I call to account—prod and correct and guide so that they'll live at their best. Up on your feet, then! About face! Run after God! Look at me. I stand at the door. I knock. If you hear me call and open the door, I'll come right in and sit down to supper with you. Conquerors will sit alongside me at the head table, just as I, having conquered, took the place of honor at the side of my Father. That's my gift to the conquerors! Are your ears awake? Listen. Listen to the Wind Words, the Spirit blowing through the churches.

Revelation 3:19-22

Both of these intense assessments are followed by the promises given above. If we respond by finding our feet, turning around, and running after God, we will look and see Him knocking at the door. If we open, He will come in!

Our response changes His response to us. No longer does Jesus call us desperate, passionless, stale, nauseating, pitiful, naked, blind, homeless people…He calls us *conquerors*!

16 | As a group or individually, fashion a prayer out of scripture that expresses our need for this makeover.

_____

_____

_____

_____

_____

Balancing the Load

That our sons may be as plants grown up in their youth; that our daughters may be as pillars, sculptured in palace style.

Psalm 144:12 NKJV

17 | Do you feel this is currently an accurate picture of what the Church looks like?

_____

a. Are both genders carrying their load, or is the distribution of weight a bit uneven?

_____

_____

18 | Highlight the words that define *pillar* for you:

Support	Column	Post	Mast
Prop	Stake	Leader	

Your own words _____

a. Do any of these words describe the merely decorative or superfluous?

_____

You've all been to the stadium and seen the athletes race. Everyone runs; one wins. Run to win. All good athletes train hard. They do it for a gold medal that tarnishes and fades. You're after one that's gold eternally. I don't know about you, but I'm running hard for the finish line. I'm giving it everything I've got. No sloppy living for me! I'm staying alert and in top condition. I'm not going to get caught napping, telling everyone else all about it and then missing out myself.

1 Corinthians 9:24-27

19 | Drawing on the admonition from the scripture above, list 4 things we must we do to win:

1. _____

2. _____

3. _____

4. _____

Setting Aside Former Limitations

20 | Let's talk about your competitive sports involvement. List the sports you've participated in:

_____

_____

_____

a. Why did you join a team?

_____

_____

b. How did you perform?

_____

_____

c. Did you have the team or yourself in mind?

_____

To arise a lioness and bring contribution to the pride, we must become focused.

My dear friends, this is now the second time I've written to you, both letters reminders to hold your minds in a state of undistracted attention.

2 Peter 3:1

You and I are responsible for holding our minds at attention. No one else can hold your mind but you. You determine what you will attend to. It is one of the ways you develop strength. Peter goes on to explain why this is so important and yet such a challenge.

Keep in mind what the holy prophets said, and the command of our Master and Savior that was passed on by your apostles. (verse 2)

Deposit in your mind what the prophets, our Master, and the apostles have told us.

First off, you need to know that in the last days, mockers are going to have a heyday. Reducing everything to the level of their puny feelings, they'll mock, "So what's happened to the promise of his Coming? Our ancestors are dead and buried, and everything's going on just as it has from the first day of creation. Nothing's changed." (verses 3-4)

Beware of mockers!

They conveniently forget that long ago all the galaxies and this very planet were brought into existence out of watery chaos by God's word. Then God's word brought the chaos back in a flood that destroyed the world. The current galaxies and earth are fuel for the final fire. God is poised, ready to speak his word again, ready to give the signal for the judgment and destruction of the desecrating skeptics.

2 Peter 3:5-7

21 | According to the above verses, what is our greatest threat?

_____

_____

Pride Play

Find a nature trail, beautiful bridge, or path through your neighborhood. Get outside, shake off the dust of the day, take a deep breath, and enjoy a walk among sisters. Discuss the limitations you or others have placed on your life and determine to leave those things on the path behind.

Room for Reflection...

_____

_____

_____

_____

Legend Lioness

"I am not afraid. I was born to do this."[4]

Joan of Arc, military leader who believed herself to be on a God-given mission to liberate northern France from the English.

LIONESS LESSONS

- ⊠ Worship and develop that marvelous, fearsome wonder to its maximum capacity.

- ⊠ Don't be content to lower your goal to merely "looking good"; develop the muscle you need to bear some weight, lift others, and "do good."

- ⊠ Don't be skinny fat or fat fat. Glorify God with your body by shifting your focus to developing strength rather than losing weight.

- ⊠ Use seasons of hardship or captivity to your advantage (like the imprisoned Sarah) and develop your strength.

- ⊠ Exchange invisible for invincible.

- ⊠ Allow Jesus to assess your life in light of the Word.

- ⊠ Run to win, train hard, give it all you've got, don't live sloppy, stay alert and in peak condition. No napping and missing out!

Pride Purpose

Do not fear your strength; temper, master, and develop it!

PROWESS
You are fearfully and wonderfully made.

FIERCE FACTS
- Lions are the only social cats, living in groups called prides.[5]
- A pride comprises of interrelated females and one to four adult males.[6]

Prayer Roar

This day, regardless of how I look or feel, I choose to echo the declaration, "I am fearfully and wonderfully made." God's work in me is marvelous. I am stunning; but, more than just looking good, I choose to develop the strength to "do good." I am ready to bear some weight and carry my load because rather than being busy, I will build. I will shift my focus to gaining strength and allow hardship to remake me invincible in Him. I embrace my strength and choose to run to win, train hard, give it my all, stay alert, and not get sloppy with the Word of God or the seasons of my life.

IMPRESSIONS

(1) *Peter McWilliams Quotes* (http://thinkexist.com/quotation/our_thoughts_create_our_reality-where_we_put_our/332835.html, retrieved 11-16-2010). (2) *Gifts of Speech*, "Nobel Lecture by Betty Williams" (http://gos.sbc.edu/w/bwilliams.html, retrieved 11-18-2010). (3) http://www.quotationspage.com/quote/31896.html, retrieved 11-16-2010. (4) *Women Who Changed the World: Fifty Inspirational Women Who Shaped History* (Millers Point NSW, Australia: Pier 9, 2006), p. 26. (5) *Interesting Facts about Lions* (http://ezinearticles.com/?Interesting-Facts-About-Lions&id=869621, retrieved 11-11-2010). (6) Ibid.

IMPRESSIONS

STRENGTH IS FOR SERVICE 5

Finally one of the lionesses decided to go for it. Her hunger won out over her hesitation. She boldly crossed the line and approached the slain buck. At the halfway point she glanced back to her sister, as though inviting her to join her on the other side of the fence.

[page 78]

1 | What did the story of the lionesses and their lion speak to you?

_____

_____

_____

_____

a. What previously fenced-off areas are now open to you?

_____

_____

_____

b. Will your hunger (or the hunger of others) win out over your hesitation?

_____

_____

Helping Those Who Falter

2 | What goodness is God asking you to bring back to others?

_____

_____

_____

_____

Those of us who are strong and able in the faith need to step in and lend a hand to those who falter, and not just do what is most convenient for us. Strength is for service, not status. Each one of us needs to look after the good of the people around us, asking ourselves, "How can I help?"

Romans 15:1-2

3 | What is *currently* an area of strength in your life that you could use to help others?

_____

_____

a. How often do we ask people how we can help? Or do we usually do what we are comfortable with and tell them how we are willing to help?

_____

_____

_____

"It would be considered a theft on our part if we didn't give to someone in greater need than we are."

St. Francis of Assisi

b. How do you need help right now?

_____

_____

_____

_____

_____

c. Who can you encourage right now?

_____

_____

_____

Lifting Religion's Weight

4 | Did you connect with my hesitation—and even fear—of speaking to mixed-gender audiences?

_____

Believe me,
you cannot
please everyone,
so obey God.

The very woman who used to tell me it was wrong for me to speak to a mixed-gender audience now travels and speaks to mixed-gender audiences. (Yet it is quite possible she still thinks it is wrong for me and right for her, because religion is inconsistent and rarely makes sense.)

So the choice becomes: *Are we going to obey God and serve His people in the process, or are we going to obey people and dishonor God's directive?*

5 | What are the areas of life you tend to falter in because you are hesitant?

_____

_____

_____

a. Is anyone served by your hesitancy?

_____

None of us should apologize for stewarding well what God has entrusted to our care.

6 | Honestly, are you afraid of being confident because it might be mistaken for arrogance or stepping out beyond your place?

_____

_____

Let me just settle this for you. Because we are in a season of many transitions for women, you will be accused of stepping out of place. Therefore, you might as well just choose to walk confidently. You cannot let let fear rule or guide you!

> *I prayed to the Lord, and he answered me. He freed me from all my fears. Those who look to him for help will be radiant with joy; no shadow of shame will darken their faces.*
>
> Psalm 34:4-5 NLT

Shame and religion tend to introduce shadows into the equation and mask our radiance.

> *Instead of giving you God's Law as food and drink by which you can banquet on God, they package it in bundles of rules, loading you down like pack animals. They seem to take pleasure in watching you stagger under these loads, and wouldn't think of lifting a finger to help. Their lives are perpetual fashion shows, embroidered prayer shawls one day and flowery prayers the next. They love to sit at the head table at church dinners, basking in the most prominent positions, preening in the radiance of public flattery, receiving honorary degrees, and getting called 'Doctor' and 'Reverend.'*
>
> Matthew 23:4-7

There was to be a banquet, not a bundle. Jesus goes on to explain the elitism of the degrees, titles, prayer shawls, and decorative prayers. The longer I live, the more I realize God is very organic—He appreciates the raw and simple.

7 | We may not have prayer shawls, but are we still burdening others and making a show of our own religiosity? If so, in what ways?

_____

_____

_____

a. Why do leaders do this?

_____

_____

b. Why do we do this?

_____

_____

If God's law was meant to strengthen us, how much more the gift?

Jesus continues with this admonishment of how leaders should be postured.

> *Don't let people do that to you, put you on a pedestal like that.
> You all have a single Teacher, and you are all classmates. Don't set
> people up as experts over your life, letting them tell you what to do.
> Save that authority for God; let him tell you what to do. No one else
> should carry the title of 'Father'; you have only one Father, and he's in
> heaven. And don't let people maneuver you into taking charge of them.
> There is only one Life-Leader for you and them—Christ.*
>
> Matthew 23:8-10

Leaders: Don't let people put you on a pedestal; it will set you up for a fall! Don't let others make you responsible for them...this is a Moses dynamic!

Leaders and those they serve should all maintain the same posture, which is: *Who is our ultimate Life Leader?*

This does not mean there are no teachers, leaders, pastors, or authorities in your life. It just means you should not give undue power to them.

8 | Do you believe women can minister?

_____

_____

    a. Do you believe single women can minister?

_____

9 | Do we make it complicated to serve God?

_____

    a. What did Jesus do? Did He complicate or simplify the gospel?

_____

    b. What did the religious leaders of Jesus' day do? Did they complicate or simplify the gospel?

_____

10 | If the dynamic of what a leader is would change to this servant leadership model, do you think more women would be comfortable with the concept of women as leaders?

_____

What is your mother?
A lioness among lions!
Ezekiel 19:2 NLT

11 | In what way(s) could you likewise be a lioness among lions?

_____

_____

_____

_____

    a. Are you presently a lioness among lions?

_____

⊠ HUNT QUEST ⊠

Hope to the Hopeless

I found it amazing that I discovered dreams amid the overwhelming addictions and despair on the streets of Cambodia, Thailand, and India.

12 | When was the last time you asked someone what he or she wanted for his or her life?

_____

_____

a. When was the last time you were part of fulfilling someone else's dream?

_____

_____

_____

b. Who needs you to invite them to dream?

_____

_____

_____

c. Who can you encourage today?

_____

_____

A Lioness Truth

I already mentioned that we are a people in transition. I want to revisit what the sister lionesses modeled so beautifully at the beginning of this chapter.

The lionesses chose to behave in a way that honored the mighty lion that one day would be, rather than respond to the immaturity of the one who cowered in the bush before them. Love believes the best. This often means we can choose to respond to the worst or the best in the behavior of those around us.

I want to be surrounded by people who see my potential—not ignore my problems or current challenges, but respond to who I can be rather than who I am. No one in my life has done this better than my husband. Honor causes everyone to flourish!

13 | How many of us model this lioness attitude? In what ways can you return goodness and honor to those now faltering?

_____

_____

_____

_____

14 | What do you think about this concept? *Taking less now does not mean having less in our future.*

_____

_____

_____

_____

a. What does it speak to you?

_____

_____

_____

Strength is for service, not status.
Romans 15:2

15 | How does this fly in the face of our nation's culture?

_____

_____

_____

a. Is this what we have modeled in our church culture?

_____

b. How can you be part of changing this perception?

_____

_____

Rise Up for Excellent Service

16 | Define the word *service*:

_____

_____

_____

> *Don't imagine us leaders to be something we aren't. We are servants of Christ, not his masters. We are guides into God's most sublime secrets, not security guards posted to protect them. The requirements for a good guide are reliability and accurate knowledge. It matters very little to me what you think of me, even less where I rank in popular opinion. I don't even rank myself. Comparisons in these matters are pointless.*
>
> 1 Corinthians 4:1-3

17 | What do you think the following statement means? *We are guides into God's most sublime secrets, not security guards posted to protect them.*

_____

_____

_____

_____

18 | Why is it important to not consider your rank in popularity as you pursue being a good guide?

_____

_____

_____

Legend Lioness

"When I was growing up I thought a woman could have it all and now I find that, yes, a woman can have it all – but she has to be prepared to pay the price."[2]

Benazir Bhutto, 1st woman to lead a Muslim country, advocate for the improvement of conditions for women and the underprivileged in Pakistan. Sadly, she was assassinated December 27, 2007.

19 | Why are comparisons pointless?

_____

_____

_____

> "The best way to find yourself is to lose yourself in the service of others."[3]
> Mohandas Gandhi

20 | What do you think it means to have a reach that is both generous and noble?

_____

_____

_____

_____

_____

_____

_____

> Dear, dear Corinthians, I can't tell you how much I long for you to enter this wide-open, spacious life. We didn't fence you in. The smallness you feel comes from within you. Your lives aren't small, but you're living them in a small way. I'm speaking as plainly as I can and with great affection. Open up your lives. Live openly and expansively!
> 2 Corinthians 6:11-13

21 | What does this scripture speak to you?

_____

_____

_____

a. What does it mean to live in a small way?

_____

_____

_____

> My dear children, you come from God and belong to God...for the Spirit in you is far stronger than anything in the world.
> 1 John 4:4

22 | If we really, truly believe 1 John 4:4 and couple it with the realization
that our strength is for service, what will we look like?

_____

_____

_____

a. Write a few words to describe this crossing over the threshold.

_____

_____

_____

Pride Play

Taking the charge of Romans 15:2, decide as a company of lioness sisters
what person, or group of people, you know in your immediate world with
whom your strength can make a difference – and do it!

Room for Reflection...

_____

_____

_____

_____

LIONESS LESSONS

⊠ A life of worship should be a banquet, not a burden.

⊠ Be a lioness among lions.

⊠ Help people dream again.

⊠ Taking less now does not mean having less in the future.

⊠ We are guides, not security guards.

⊠ Any smallness you feel comes from within you; it is not from
God.

Pride Purpose

Strength is for service, not for status.
(Romans 15:2)

PROWESS
Acts of honor
are never lost
in translation.

FIERCE FACTS

- The average reign for male lions over a pride is two to three years.[4]
- Lion cubs are born with spots, but as they mature, the spots fade. Since cubs are the most vulnerable to predators when they are young, the spots may give camouflage until they are old enough to either get away or begin hunting themselves.[5]

Prayer Roar

I present my strength for your service, God, and I refuse to allow anyone to put me in a position of status. I choose to serve and lift others by asking, "How can I help?" I will change the way I look at my life of worship. It is a banquet of refreshing and strength, not a draining burden. Show me how to be a lioness among lions and in the process, raise up others in their strengths and encourage them to dream again. I know acts of honor are never lost in translation, so I look to my future with hope because taking less now does not mean having less in my future. I am a guide, not a guard. I live to bring people in, not to keep them out. Enlarge my life!

(1) Carol Kelly-Gangi, ed. *Saint Francis of Assisi: His Essential Wisdom* (New York, NY: Fall River Press, 2010), p. 56. (2) *Women Who Changed the World: Fifty Inspirational Women Who Shaped History* (Millers Point NSW, Australia: Pier 9, 2006), p. 186. (3) *Mohandas Gandhi Quotes* (http://www.brainyquote.com/quotes/quotes/m/mohandasga150725.html, retrieved 11-16-2010). (4) *Lion Pictures and Facts* (http://fohn.net/lion-pictures-facts/lion-3.html, retrieved 11-30-2010). (5) Ibid.

IMPRESSIONS

IMPRESSIONS

UNDER THE SAME MISSION 6

"Every time we liberate a woman, we liberate a man."[1]
Margaret Mead

1 | Do you think this statement is true? If so, why does freeing a woman
release a man? If you disagree with her observation, why?

_____

_____

_____

_____

In this chapter you are going to notice that I've chosen quite a few quotes
from Archbishop Desmond Tutu. My reasoning was this: If he could
pastor the racial reconciliation of a nation, then perhaps he would have
invaluable insight into gender reconciliation. This issue is a challenge we
must all undertake. It is my prayer that what we learn individually on our
journey to equality will free both men and women on their journeys.

Healthy lions and lionesses know they *need* each other if they are to
flourish rather than merely survive. The key words here are *healthy, need,*
and *flourish.* It is healthy to admit we need others; it is healing for *both
genders* to acknowledge this truth. We need the men, and they need us.
Flourishing requires the involvement of both male and female. The alpha
lion wants to be surrounded by strong, healthy lionesses. He is wise
enough to staff his weaknesses.

"Differences are not intended to separate, to alienate. We are different precisely in order to realize our need of one another."[2]

Archbishop Desmond Tutu

The lion does not oppress the lioness in order to showcase his power. He has already won the challenge by establishing dominance over the other males. This show of strength gives him the right to lead the pride of lionesses. He now resides with them to empower and protect them so they in turn will establish his legacy in strength.

There is no need to dominate, male or female, when those around you know you would do everything in your power to protect them.

Submission: Under Mission

Our lives are filled with missions. Throughout the course of life, a mission may change with the seasons.

For example: When you are a student, the school's mission is to educate, and your mission is to learn. Moving into the marketplace, there are different missions. Businesses sell or provide goods or services in exchange for money. Churches are on a mission to build the lives of their members and reach out to their communities to save and disciple the lost. In addition to making money and creating fame, Hollywood has a mission to influence and entertain. Regardless of what drives the mission, it is tied to some purpose.

Individuals who do not live on purpose wander aimlessly.

God made us on purpose, for purpose. He was very intentional in how He uniquely crafted you. He did not have a lesser purpose in mind for you because you are a woman. Your purpose is uniquely powerful and feminine. Men and women both have a mission. You have purpose whether you are married or single.

When a man and woman decide to *do life together*, their lives should likewise reflect God's purpose for marriage. Marriage is two becoming one; it is a life-long dance. The man lays down his life and loves his wife as Christ loves the Church. The woman, in turn, respects her husband and multiplies his life by doing him good and not harm.

Marriage is not a power struggle—it is a power union. It is built by two people who are in covenant and committed to God, who honor His statutes with their life choices and live so vibrantly in Him that others are drawn to His light in their lives.

> *"Life has taught us that love does not consist in gazing at each other, but in looking outward together in the same direction."*[3]
>
> Antoine de Saint-Exupéry

2 | If you are single, write your individual life mission:

_____

_____

_____

_____

a. Married women, list your family mission:

_____

_____

_____

_____

3 | Do these missions fall under God's mission for us as His representatives?

_____

> *God put the world square with himself through the Messiah, giving the world a fresh start by offering forgiveness of sins. God has **given us the task of telling everyone what he is doing.** We're Christ's representatives. God uses us to persuade men and women to drop their differences and enter into God's work of making things right between them.*
>
> 2 Corinthians 5:19-20

I can't think of a better description of God's mission for us! He wants us (men and women) to work *together* as persuasive influencers, using the medium of our lives to tell other men and women to drop their differences and enter in or cross the threshold into what God is doing to make things right in our earth.

Now the question arises: *What is our focus?* Are we telling people what God is doing? Or are we too busy telling them what they can and cannot do?

4 | What is your focus?

_____

_____

_____

a. Is the gospel we now preach persuasive and influential, or is it unconvincing and restrictive?

_____

_____

I say "unconvincing" because too often people question our gospel due to the lack of transformation in the way we treat one another. God is for conflict resolution, and it begins with a fresh start for everyone.

> *Now we look inside, and what we see is that anyone united with the Messiah gets a fresh start, is created new. The old life is gone; a new life burgeons! Look at it! All this comes from the God who settled the relationship between us and him, and then called us to settle our relationships with each other.*
>
> 2 Corinthians 5:17-18

Never doubt that settling the battle of the sexes is a God-calling.

✦ HUNT QUEST ✦

Twitter Twist

I have included, again, my comment that received nearly 500 responses on Facebook. Please remember the majority of the comments were in agreement and highly favorable. There were but a few *women* who were furious that I might suggest women can lead.

"Gender alone does not qualify a man to lead, just as gender alone should not disqualify a woman. Virtue qualifies both male and female."

5 | What is your reaction to this statement?

Strongly Agree--Strongly Disagree

   a. Why do you take that position?

       _____

       _____

       _____

       _____

6 | Write your own definition of a leader.

_____

_____

_____

_____

   a. According to your definition, are you a leader?

       _____

   b. Give an example of someone who has been a leader in your life.

       _____

       _____

       _____

       _____

7 | Review the list of leadership qualifications in 1 Timothy 3:1-13 that Paul passed onto Timothy (also on pages 98-99 in *Lioness Arising*).

   a. What do you think the emphasis of this passage is—gender or qualifications?

       _____

b. Why would Paul give a list of leadership qualifications for the women if women were not supposed to be leaders?

_____

_____

_____

_____

8 | Why is it that women can serve in leadership everywhere but the church?

_____

_____

_____

_____

a. What arguments have you heard to support this?

_____

_____

_____

b. What scriptures can you find to support this?

_____

_____

_____

_____

Sexist Attitudes

9 | Have you experienced a sexist attitude...

a. at work?

_____

b. at church?

_____

c. Write down the incident(s) and how it made you feel.

_____

_____

_____

_____

_____

_____

10 | During prayer or personal study, has God ever spoken to you in a sexist or discriminatory manner?

_____

11 | Has God ever asked you to do something you imagined you couldn't because you are a woman? If so, what was it?

_____

_____

_____

_____

12 | Do you believe women were equally redeemed by Jesus' finished work on the cross?

_____

13 | It is only natural to have a dynamic of submission toward one husband, but has "submission" ever been used against you outside your marriage simply because you are a woman? If so, how?

_____

_____

_____

14 | How do you feel when you see men and their roles devalued?

Vindicated   Sad   I think it is funny

I do not notice men being devalued

a. Who are you more prone to laugh at? Men Women

b. Who are you more prone to laugh with? Men Women

"I cannot be opposed to racism, in which people are discriminated against as a result of something about which they can do nothing—their skin color—and then accept with equanimity the gross injustice of penalizing others for something else they can do nothing about—their gender."[4]
Archbishop Desmond Tutu

The Feminine Divine

I know this is edgy content, but it is a very real concern. Rather than react we need to be aware, go to the root cause of this migration away from patriarchal, and realize where we stand, lest we fall.

15 | Were you aware of goddess worship? If so, in what ways, and where have you seen indications of it?

_____

_____

_____

_____

a. Why do you think this has gained prominence?

_____

_____

_____

16 | How did you feel after reading Sue Monk Kidd's angst on pages 102-103 in *Lioness Arising*?

_____

_____

_____

_____

17 | Have you heard the reasoning that the woman was the first to sin and the last to be created?

_____

a. How did it make you feel?

_____

_____

_____

_____

b. Was it used to limit female involvement?

_____

18 | Do you think God is still looking for someone to blame for the fall, or were we all at fault?

_____

_____

_____

For there is no difference; for all have sinned and fall short of the glory of God, being justified freely by His grace through the redemption that is in Christ Jesus.
Romans 3:23-24 NKJV

19 | Did Jesus take on the sin of both men and women, or just men?

_____

If either gender argues that they are in some way less guilty, they undermine their need for God's mercy. But for the sake of argument...

If you sin without knowing what you're doing, God takes that into account. But if you sin knowing full well what you're doing, that's a different story entirely.
Romans 2:12

20 | In light of this passage, how do you see Adam and Eve's sin?

_____

_____

_____

Ultimately, God alone redeems in order for both to flourish, so it is silly to imply that either the male or female is somehow less in the redemptive plan of God.

21 | When there is a question, where should we go to find our answers?

Our leaders   The Bible   Our life experiences

A Quest for Divine Purpose

22 | How did you feel after reading the excerpts from _A Woman's Worth_ on pages 104-105 in _Lioness Arising_?

_____

_____

23 | Is there anything in scripture that recommends we pray to Mary, or any person outside of God for that matter?

_____

a.   Why would praying to an unnamed spirit be dangerous?

_____

_____

24 | How does calling ourselves "goddesses" overstep our human boundaries?

_____

_____

As awful as the disrespect and devaluing of the feminine has been, the answer is not found in disrespecting and devaluing men. Never allow your broken femininity to drive you to a place of worshiping the feminine. God alone deserves our worship. Like Christ, let us strip ourselves and become servants. Listen to Paul as he pleads with the Philippian church:

> "Arrogance really comes from insecurity, and in the end our feeling that we are bigger than others is really the flip side of our feeling that we are smaller than others."[5]
>
> Archbishop Desmond Tutu

> If you've gotten anything at all out of following Christ, if his love has made any difference in your life, if being in a community of the Spirit means anything to you, if you have a heart, if you care—then do me a favor: **Agree with each other, love each other, be deep-spirited friends.** Don't push your way to the front; don't sweet-talk your way to the top. Put yourself aside, and help others get ahead. Don't be obsessed with getting your own advantage. Forget yourselves long enough to lend a helping hand.
>
> Philippians 2:1-4

Lovely ones, knowing that we are God's daughters should not change our stance to that of the arrogant and haughty. It is only when we know who we truly are that we can live as Paul describes. We are ambassadors and servants. If we lived like this, we would not be accused of being "so unlike our Christ."

> "I like your Christ. I do not like your Christians. They are so unlike your Christ."[6]
>
> Mohandas Gandhi

Lioness sisters, let's begin to change that perception. This transformation must first take place among us if it will ever reach beyond us.

> "In the act of forgiveness we are declaring our faith in the future of a relationship and in the capacity of the wrongdoer to change."[7]
>
> Archbishop Desmond Tutu

Both genders are allies and guardians, not enemies and gods! Lionesses know the lion is not their enemy. *Together* the lion and the lioness join forces to fight off their common enemies.

The Value of Strong Women

While I was writing this book, I shared this comment on both Twitter and Facebook:

Strengthening, valuing, and empowering women does not weaken, devalue, or diminish men—there's love, honor, and respect enough for all.

When it posted to Facebook, one man told me I needed to learn "my place." I showed his comment to my husband. John was so disturbed that he reposted the comment. It is interesting to note that no one told John to know "his place."

25 | Review the breakdown of 1 Corinthians 11:10-12.

a. Do you think we read too much into the differences between men and women?

_____

_____

b. Do you believe the sexes are interdependent?

_____

_____

c. Do you feel Paul balanced both sides of the scales?

_____

_____

d. Does the fact that "everything comes from God" settle anything for you? If so, what?

_____

_____

_____

"In the Last Days," God says, "I will pour out my Spirit
on every kind of people: Your sons will prophesy, also your daughters;
Your young men will see visions, your old men dream dreams.
When the time comes, I'll pour out my Spirit
On those who serve me, men and women both, and they'll prophesy."

Acts 2:17-18

26 | What does this passage speak to you about the last-day role of men and women?

_____

_____

_____

_____

_____

_____

_____

_____

> *"For true reconciliation is a deeply personal matter. It can happen only between persons who assert their own personhood and who acknowledge and respect that of others."[8]*
>
> Archbishop Desmond Tutu

Pride Play

Consider the people in your life with whom you're on a mission. Whether they are male, female, husbands, leaders, pastors, or friends, discuss how you can intentionally encourage and strengthen them this week. When you gather again, share what happened.

Room for Reflection...

_____

_____

_____

_____

_____

_____

LIONESS LESSONS

- Good leaders staff their weaknesses.

- God thinks men and women together are amazing; that is why He blesses their union!

- All have sinned and fallen short…period.

- Men and women were equally redeemed.

- God alone deserves our worship.

- Both genders are allies and guardians, not enemies and gods!

- Don't read too much into the differences between men and women because everything comes from God.

- In the last days, God will have His say!

Pride Purpose

Marriage is not a power struggle—it is a power union.

> **PROWESS**
> Our differences highlight our need for one another.

FIERCE FACTS

- Lions do not like competition and frequently attack and kill fellow predators like leopards, hyenas, and cheetahs.[9]
- The Swahili word for lion is *simba*. It also means king, strong, and aggressive.[10]

Prayer Roar

I pray my release means release for others, male and female. Help me to always remember that marriage is a union, not a battle. Let me recognize the gender differences as the affirmation of our need for each other. I need the men in my world to be all that You created them to be. God, bless the dwellings of unity in my life. We all need redemption, and You alone are worthy of my worship. I will stop being contentious and reading too much into gender differences because You have ultimate preeminence. May You have Your say in my life!

IMPRESSIONS

(1) *Margaret Mead Quotes* (http://womenshistory.about.com/cs/quotes/a/qu_margaretmead_2. htm, retrieved 11-18-2010). (2) Archbishop Desmond Tutu, *Believe* (Boulder, CO: Blue Mountain Press, 2007), p. 51. (3) *Antoine de Saint-Exupery Quotes* (http://thinkexist.com/quotation/ life_has_taught_us_that_love_does_not_consist_in/174000.html, retrieved 11-18-2010). (4) See note 2, p. 52. (5) Ibid., p. 91. (6) *Mohandas Gandhi Quotes* (http://www.brainyquote.com/quotes/ quotes/m/mohandasga107529.html, retrieved 11-18-2010). (7) See note 2, p. 79. (8) Ibid., p. 81. (9) *Interesting Facts About Lions* (http://ezinearticles.com/?expert=Omer_Ashraf, retrieved 11-11-2010). (10) *The Jungle Store* (http://www.thejunglestore.com/Lion-Facts, retrieved 11-15-2010).

IMPRESSIONS

GREET AND GROOM 7

"For attractive lips, speak words of kindness.
For lovely eyes, seek out the good in people.
For a slim figure, share your food with the hungry.
For beautiful hair, let a child run his or her fingers through it once a day.
For poise, walk with the knowledge that you never walk alone."

Sam Levenson & Audrey Hepburn

I love this quote! How beautiful we would all be if we lived this as a daily routine. When I found it, I had to share it!

1 | What is your favorite line in this quote?

_____

_____

    a. Do you believe it is true? Why?

_____

_____

_____

_____

    b. Which suggestion is the most challenging?

_____

_____

2 | What is the purpose of the lioness's greeting?

_____

_____

_____

_____

When lionesses gather they not only greet, but they also groom. Isn't it fascinating that when they make face-to-face contact, the scent glands above their eyes release the scent of the pride?

Once they know they belong to one another, there is acceptance and an invitation into their fold. They are a related company with related children. Whether they are greeting a cub or a sister, they are saying:

"You belong with us. You are welcome to be at ease among us and discover your strengths as you grow among us. There is pro-vision and safety for you here in the pride."

So I greet you now in a similar way from the book of Jude:

Relax, everything's going to be all right; rest, everything's coming together; open your hearts, love is on the way!

(1:2)

It may be all falling apart "out there," but "in here," be secure and at ease. Everything is coming together because love is bringing us together!

3 | Why do we greet one another?

_____

_____

_____

_____

a. Has the greeting lost some of its power in our modern translation?

_____

b. Is it more of a preliminary or an essential?

_____

c. If it became an essential, how would it posture us all differently?

_____

_____

_____

When lionesses greet and groom each other, they are showing acceptance and belonging. As God's daughters, we must do the same with the people in our lives. This can easily begin with our patterns at home and work its way outside.

Greeting and Grooming Your Kids

4 | How affectionate was the house you grew up in?

1-------------------------------10

How affectionate is your household?

1-------------------------------10

How affectionate are you with your friends?

1-------------------------------10

a. Do you wish your home was more affectionate?

_____

b. Do you wish you were more comfortable with being affectionate?

_____

Establish a daily rhythm of greeting in your home. If you don't already have one, then create one now. Your kids, especially teenagers, may resist at first, but don't quit! Figure out a way.

If a child who used to embrace becomes resistant to your hugs, find out why. You don't want to allow your children to get comfortable pulling away from you. Continue to greet your kids when they become adults. Your affection serves as a reminder that they will always belong to your family; this gives them security.

5 | List some ways you can immediately introduce or reintroduce affection into your home. (You could start with something as simple as a note or a snack after school.)

_____

_____

_____

_____

_____

_____

Greeting Each Other

Greet one another with a holy embrace. All the brothers and sisters here say hello. The amazing grace of the Master, Jesus Christ, the extravagant love of God, the intimate friendship of the Holy Spirit, be with all of you.

2 Corinthians 13:12-14

Greeters are great, but we can't let them do what we are charged to do: greet and embrace. This requires both time and intent.

6 | To move toward this, let's be honest: Are you comfortable greeting people at church?

_____

7 | How comfortable are you with introductions and greetings?

I love meeting people!   It feels awkward.

I'm too busy trying to get my kids into or out of the nursery!

Where there is greeting, embrace, and grooming, there is an opportunity for God-ideas and strategies!

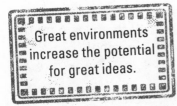

Great environments increase the potential for great ideas.

Here's another "greet and groom" from Paul:

I'm not writing all this as a neighborhood scold just to make you feel rotten. I'm writing as a father to you, my children. I love you and want you to grow up well, not spoiled. There are a lot of people around who can't wait to tell you what you've done wrong, but there aren't many fathers willing to take the time and effort to help you grow up.

1 Corinthians 4:14-15

Grooming requires time and effort because growth requires time and effort.

8 | Do you have anyone to speak into your life in this manner?

_____

   a. How important is this kind of input?

_____

_____

9 | Who is currently grooming you to grow?

_____

   a. Whom are you currently grooming?

_____

_____

It is important—no, imperative—that you have someone who speaks into your life in this manner, someone who guides your growth, and that you have those you are growing up.

> *"You must learn from the mistakes of others. You can't possibly live long enough to make them all yourself."*[3]
>
> Sam Levenson

You may argue, "I have too much need. I can't groom anyone else!" Then let them learn from your mistakes; that's what I've done!

Grooming Each Other

There are some areas of life and hygiene in which self-grooming works. There are other areas that are best left to others, or even to the professionals.

For example: It is fine for me to trim my own bangs; but with vision in only one eye, an all-over haircut would be a challenge. I have also realized coloring my own hair can be dangerous. You see, I am easily distracted, which means I forget how long I have left the color on. There have been multiple occasions when I have ended up with Joan Jett-black.

I have a Yorkie, who is definitely incapable of grooming herself, but we all know when she is in need. She begins to do some embarrassing antics. (No need for an explanation; anyone who has a dog like this will understand.) We know it is time to help her because she cannot help herself.

We are in fact "one Body." If you are in need of grooming and are doing some embarrassing things, I likewise am in need. What looks bad on you looks bad on me. Likewise, what looks bad on me makes you look bad!

Now let's bring this home a bit. Have you ever watched the Style Network's show *How Do I Look?* Well, basically this is it:

> A group of friends work with a stylist to remake a friend they love and care about. First they go through her current clothes and challenge how well it communicates who she is. Often the woman who is the project is sending mixed messages. They have the host and a guest stylist (professionals) there to support them in their quest of helping a sister. There are lots of tears as the outdated, ridiculous, and immodest are taken away. With the old out of the way, the friends and stylist each go shopping for her. They compile three collections they feel express her. These are whole packages that include hair, makeup, and wardrobe ranging from casual to evening attire. Once the favorite collection is chosen,

the subject of the makeover is transformed and presented before her friends and family. I do not think I have watched an episode and remained tearless. It captures how we should approach one another.

We need to be lioness women who have each others' backsides on this one. We cannot imagine that another sister's rough patch is not our own. If something as simple as a clothing swap, laughter, and some makeup can lighten the mood...let's do it!

Let's take this deeper. Because we are connected, we are accountable to and for one another.

10 | On a much larger scale, who is the ultimate Groomer of all?

_____

   a. How does He groom us?

_____

_____

_____

_____

You are already clean because of the word which I have spoken to you.

John 15:3 NKJV

He actually greeted us and called us His own before we were clean! He loved us first and took our filth on Himself so we might be made white as snow.

According to John 15:3, we are clean because the Word has washed us. It is also capable of untangling our messy issues. There is no need to immerse ourselves daily in a whole body baptism for a spiritual cleansing. When I was first born again, I prayed the sinner's prayer every service in the belief that the failures of that day or week might have disqualified me.

Once a child is adopted, their next infraction does not send them back to the orphanage. They belong. There is only the need to wash away the dirt of that day's journey, and with the washing comes refreshing.

11 | Since we don't literally do the dynamic of the foot washing any longer, what is a ritual that would express the same warmth and invitation to come in, leave your day behind, and be at ease? List some ideas:

_____

_____

Then, there is the issue of the matted and tangled areas of life:

An open rebuke is better than hidden love! Wounds from a sincere friend are better than many kisses from an enemy. A person who is full refuses honey, but even bitter food tastes sweet to the hungry.

Proverbs 27:5-7 NLT

Many of us have heard this referenced. What does it mean by an "open rebuke"? Well, I have experienced the "closed rebuke" before, and I bet you have too. It is when people correct you behind your back. When people correct you in your absence, you need to question the sincerity of their rebuke. They may even be correct in what they say, but it does not help you grow unless you are included in the process. It usually hurts your growth process, because when people speak about you behind your back, they set you up to react defensively. The face-to-face "open rebuke" of a sincere or genuine friend gives a person the chance to respond and therefore grow.

I want the kind of friends who come to me first. This means I need to be the kind of friend who does the same.

☒ HUNT QUEST ☒

Holiness, Not Hygiene

My concern, you understand, is holiness, not hygiene.

John 13:10

In reference to the foot wash, Jesus said His bottom-line concern was holiness, NOT hygiene! A rebuke washes feet without questioning the hygiene of the rest of the person's body or their right to belong to the body. The only one Jesus called unclean was Judas, who not only betrayed him, but was also filled with greed.

So clean the inside by giving gifts to the poor,
and you will be clean all over.

Luke 11:41 NLT

12 | Generosity to those who cannot return your kindness is the ultimate internal cleanse. Let's pause... To whom can you, as an individual or group, give gifts of time, money, or service in order to see this type of clean up happen? (This is different than paying your tithe.)

_____

_____

_____

The Ultimate Grooming Act

Then turning to the woman, but speaking to Simon, he said,
"Do you see this woman? I came to your home; you provided
no water for my feet, but she rained tears on my feet and dried them
with her hair. You gave me no greeting, but from the time
I arrived she hasn't quit kissing my feet. You provided nothing
for freshening up, but she has soothed my feet with perfume. Impressive,
isn't it? She was forgiven many, many sins, and so she is very,
very grateful. If the forgiveness is minimal, the gratitude is minimal."

Luke 7:43-47

How like our Jesus to ask, "Do you see this woman?" To be quite honest, I seriously doubt if Simon saw much else. We should realize Jesus is not addressing the obvious here; He is asking, "Do you really see this woman? Can you see her the way I see her?" Then, to underscore what He sees, He uses the actions and faith of this woman to teach one of the core gospel truths.

Jesus begins by looking at the woman and speaking to Simon and ends by looking and speaking to the woman. In these interactions, Jesus contrasts the woman's reception of Him with that of Simon.

Simon	The Woman
No Water	Rained Tears
No Greeting	Continual Kissing
No Refreshing	Soothing Perfume
Unimpressive	Impressive
Minimal Sins	Many, Many Sins
Minimal Gratitude	Very, Very Grateful
Ignored	Noticed
	Forgiven & Leaves in Peace

Simon was trying to impress the friends he had invited by hosting an invitation-only dinner with Jesus. But the unexpected and uninvited impressed our Jesus. He is seemingly unimpressed by the clean and important gathered around the table and takes notice of the unclean woman in their midst. I love this.

The choices are now before us:
Will we go where we are uninvited and rain our tears?
Will we kiss the feet of Jesus by the way we greet others?
Will we refresh others, though it is an expense to us?

13 | In what practical ways can you do this in your world of influence?

_____

_____

Lovely lioness sisters, it is time our actions again gave our glorious Lord something to brag about! Are we willing to go where we were not invited and wash feet?

Let's greet, embrace, and groom one another to do something wonderfully significant! Let us, together, be this woman!

Pride Play

Check out the show *How Do I Look?* on the Style Network (www.my-style.com/howdoilook) or any other makeover show, and get inspired! Part of the grooming process is helping each other see strengths and weaknesses—and the wardrobe shouldn't be excluded. Get into your girlfriend's closet and find the items that really look good on her and make her feel great. Remove the dated and frumpy items. Cleanse the closet! You will see there is more in there than you realized, and looking and feeling great is a step toward being a groomed woman.

LIONESS LESSONS

- ✖ The greeting has the power to say who I am to you and who you are to me.

- ✖ The embrace communicates acceptance, welcome, and inclusion.

- ✖ Face-to-face contact has the potential to release a fragrance over both lives.

- ✖ Generosity cleanses us from the inside out.

- ✖ Open rebuke happens between friends.

- ✖ You are clean because Jesus has washed you! Because He has washed us, let's wash one another.

Pride Purpose

Greeting and grooming one another strengthens our bonds and helps us to grow up and into our strengths.

PROWESS
Some areas of life are out of our line of sight and need the attention of others.

FIERCE FACTS

- Lions live in grassy plains, savannas, open woodlands, dense bush, and scrubland. The size of their territories is dependent on the size of the pride and the availability of prey.[4]
- Lions rest for up to 21 hours a day.[5]

Prayer Roar

Jesus, we are ready to do something impressive and significant for Your Body! Show me who I am so I know how to both greet and groom my sisters and brothers. I want to refresh and restore others.

IMPRESSIONS

(1) *Sam Levenson Quotes* (http://thinkexist.com/quotation/for-attractive-lips-speak-words-of-kind-ness-for/349825.html, retrieved 11-19-2010); *Audrey Hepburn Quotes* (http://www.goodreads.com/quotes/show/15618, retrieved 11-19-2010). (2) *Eleanor Roosevelt Quotes* (http://www.brainyquote.com/quotes/quotes/e/eleanorroo385439.html, retrieved 11-19-2010). (3) *Sam Levenson Quotes* (http://thinkexist.com/quotation/you_must_learn_from_the_mistakes_of_others-you/253266.html, retrieved 11-19-2010). (4) *The Jungle Store* (http://www.thejunglestore.com/Lion-Facts, retrieved 11-11-2010). (5) Ibid.

LIONESSES ARE STRATEGIC 8

"Any beast can cry over the misfortunes of its own child.
It takes mensch to weep for others' children."
Sam Levenson

I know you are wondering what "mensch" is. It is a "Yiddish" term that describes a moral ideal for all people. It represents the kind, decent, and reliable person who is not only sensitive to the needs of others but also looks for ways to help them. I don't know if the lioness cries over the misfortunes of her pride members, but I do know she looks for ways to help.

This is why we must each know our strength and develop our prowess. Without this knowledge we will be of little or no help to one another.

1 | Like the lioness, our strategy will involve three factors: timing, camouflage, and proximity. Think of a way each of these is (or should be) factored into your life…

Timing:

_____

_____

Camouflage:

_____

_____

Proximity:

_____

_____

Prowess
[noun]
1. exceptional ability, skill, or strength
2. exceptional valor or bravery.

This is a definition with two different meanings preceded by the same adjective..._exceptional_.

When one attribute is present, it makes sense that the other one is as well. You feel brave when your performance in a certain area is exceptional. I would be frightened of platform diving because my skill in that area is subpar.

2 | What ability, skill, or strength is waiting for you to make it exceptional?

_____

_____

_____

_____

3 | Where are you brave when others are frightened?

_____

_____

_____

a. What makes you want to be brave? This is likely where you will discover your prowess.

_____

_____

Prowess might say, "I don't know or do everything, but what I know, I choose to do well."

It is time you discovered what you were made to be.

So since we find ourselves fashioned into all these excellently formed and marvelously functioning parts in Christ's body, let's just go ahead and be what we were made to be, without enviously or pridefully comparing ourselves with each other, or trying to be something we aren't.

Romans 12:5

Did you catch all of this? You were fashioned to have an excellently formed and marvelously functioning part in the Body of Christ. It is time you discovered what you were made, or created, to be! Please don't compare yourself with others and rob us all of the best you! Envy sabotages strategic relationships. Pride causes multiple falls, and no one wins when we compete with one another.

4 | What is your strategic contribution and role in the pride?

_____

_____

_____

_____

_____

_____

_____

_____

To help determine this, we have included a short, fun quiz that has been customized for this safari. Discovering your functioning role should help you realize your area of contribution. We have found these types of profiles invaluable when navigating team and family dynamics and strengths. Following the quiz is information on the test in its entirety as this is merely a window.

INSTRUCTIONS: If you can answer "yes" to the given question, circle the letter (N, P, L, T). Those you cannot answer with a "yes," leave blank. *(Answer "yes" to the questions that describe you the majority of the time.)*

1. When someone gets angry at me, I... (choose only one)
   N - Tend to ignore the anger, hoping it will go away, or try to soothe the anger and bring about peace.
   P - Immediately confront the person or issue, even if it makes that person angrier.
   L - Think about it and decide if it is important enough to interrupt my plan or project.
   T - Look for ways to learn from the experience, even if it is a difficult one.

2. T - I easily and patiently give instructions without getting frustrated if it takes too long.

3. P - I generally discern or sense danger, or that something is amiss, before others do.

4. L - I often find myself in roles of leadership.

5. L - I enjoy being in an organized group in which everyone is aware of their responsibilities and roles.

6. N - I consider myself a compassionate person.

7. P - I consider myself an assertive person.

8. N - There are often times when I don't mind stopping what I'm doing to give time and affection to my husband, children, or others.

9. P - I'm not afraid to take a risk, whether personally, professionally, or for a good or exciting reason.

10. T - I believe I'm a clear communicator and others easily understand me.

11. L - I like to stay focused until I accomplish my goals.

12. T - I enjoy training and teaching others.

13. N - I often comfort others.

Scoring:

Count the number of each letter you circled and record below. *(Example: N = 2, L = 4, P= 3, T= 1; these scores indicate that you left two blank.)*

N = _____   L = _____   P = _____   T = _____

The higher you score in any letter indicates that you are stronger in that descriptive characteristic. You have aspects of all four and could be high in all four, but there will most likely be one that is higher than the rest. The most you can score in any category is 4. The following descriptions will give you more insight into how fearfully and wonderfully made you are, and how you were created by God for His specific assignment.

N = NURTURER: You are a woman of compassion, especially toward those you care about. You are accepting, understanding, affectionate, and willing to take time to show those in your life that they matter. You make a wonderful friend. Cuddling on a sofa in front of a roaring fire with your spouse or children would be an ideal way for you to spend an evening. You can be spontaneous and fun, yet you are warm and sensitive. You are a Mary.

L = LEADER: As the lioness is valuable to her pride, so are you as a leader to your family, church, or business. You are a woman of vision, able to see the big picture and how and where each person most effectively fits. You are a strategist and a planner. You willingly work under godly authority and easily lead those you have authority over. You are a Deborah.

P = PROTECTOR: As a woman, you, like the lioness, are a fierce protector of your home, your children, and those you care about. You watch over them. You (as Proverbs 31 says) "looketh well in the ways of [your] household." This means you watch over the home—what comes in and goes out in the way of friends, television, books, CDs, DVDs, e-mail, Facebook, Twitter, and whatever else time may bring. As a Protector, you watch for evil trying to infiltrate your home, and like the angel placed at the entrance to the Garden of Eden, stand guard. You are an Esther destined to protect those you love.

T = TRAINER: The woman, as a mother, is designed to be a teacher and trainer in the lives of her children. You set the tone, mood, and ambiance of your home. Like the lioness, you teach your children how to play, where to play, the boundaries of their lives, and the difference between obedience and disobedience. When your children leave the "nest," you have them ready to enter the world with confidence, knowledge, and character.

If you would like an in-depth understanding of yourself and your personal communication style, go to www.lifelanguages.com or www.kendalllife. org and take the Kendall Life Languages Profile (KLLP). There are 115 questions, which will generate a printout of approximately 20 pages. The KLLP will help you understand yourself and how to connect with those in your life. It will help you socially, professionally, and relationally. It has saved marriages and prevented divorces. (There is a charge of $45.00, but that is much cheaper than an hour of marriage counseling.) If your teenagers take it, you may understand them for the first time; even more importantly, they will understand themselves: their strengths, filters, passions, needs, and, ultimately, their purpose. Professionally, the Kendall Profile can help you find a career that lines up with your strengths and passions.

You have been entrusted with a marvelously functioning part! We desperately need everyone in their place and strength.

5 | Before reading the book, did you know lionesses did the majority of the pride hunting?

_____

   a. How did this make you feel when you found out?

     _____

     _____

     _____

     _____

6 | What is at risk if lionesses do not work as a team?

_____

_____

_____

Can you teach the lioness to stalk her prey and satisfy the appetite of her cubs as they crouch in their den, waiting hungrily in their cave?
Job 38:39-40

I love that the lioness hunt is God-taught. The young cubs wait while the mothers hunt. We obviously are not going to bring back a carcass, so let's review the definition of *hunt* and learn what God would teach us.

A Wild Chase

Hunt
[noun]
chase, search, rescue, pursuit
[verb]
chase, pursue, stalk, hound, follow, lie in wait for

7 | What are you presently hunting (searching) for?

_____

_____

_____

_____

8 | What is your current pursuit? (How are your time and energy spent?)

_____

_____

_____

_____

9 | What revelation are you waiting patiently for?

_____

_____

_____

_____

10 | Find a scripture that describes your current posture and pursuit.

_____

_____

_____

Legend Lioness

"Sister is probably the most competitive relationship within the family, but once the sisters are grown, it becomes the strongest relationship."[2]

Margaret Mead

11 | What do you think about this quote from Margaret Mead?

_____

_____

_____

_____

a. Has it proven true in your life?

_____

_____

It is certainly my prayer that as we collectively grow and mature this can be said of us.

"The chapter of the daughters (and therefore sisters) is being written right now. Tell My daughters (the sisters) to write their lives well."
I pray history will speak well of us, that it will say we knew the gravity of our day and wrote our lives with such clarity and excellence that our children arose heroes in their span of time.

Pursuing Justice

Energy and insights of justice to those who guide and decide, strength and prowess to those who guard and protect.

Isaiah 28:6

If leadership (be it governmental, legislative, church, or judicial) is to accomplish any restoration of justice in our time, it will require both insight and energy.

Justice has an energy; injustice does as well. Likewise, both have an insightful strategy. Once justice is in play, it must be guarded and protected. The perversion and twisting of what was meant to preserve justice is rampant today—so much so that at times it seems easier to do harm than good. In some countries it is easier for a child to be purchased through a pedophile ring than it is to execute a legal adoption.

Judgment will again be found on justice, and those with virtuous hearts will pursue it.
Psalm 94:15 NLT

12 | What are some ways you can pursue justice?

_____

_____

_____

13 | What are some ways you can move the children in your world out of harm's way?

_____

_____

_____

14 | Which of the following ways can you and your friends and family get involved?

Pray   Educate myself on issues near & far

Raise awareness   Educate my children

Be involved with my local school board   Give financial support

Volunteer my time & talents

15 | I have discovered that frightened people only protect their own. Why do you believe this is not expansive enough?

_____

_____

_____

16 | When you learned that lionesses plan their conceptions around optimal conditions for the cubs to war, how did that speak to you?

_____

_____

_____

_____

It is fun to share expectancy.

17 | Did you go through any pregnancies with a friend?

_____

_____

a. What did you like best about it?

_____

_____

_____

b. Did you help one another out after the babies were born?

_____

c. How did that journey feel compared to ones you did alone?

_____

_____

_____

⊠ HUNT QUEST ⊠

Because you've always stood up for me, I'm free to run and play.

Psalm 63:7

This verse highlights something key: Running and playing happens in an environment of protection—where no one is afraid of not being defended.

18 | Did you realize that like lions, humans learn what they are good at (prowess) through play?

_____

_____

19 | What recreational activities do you enjoy?

_____

_____

20 | What is an area of play you could engage in even now to develop your prowess?

_____

_____

_____

21 | Do you believe every child deserves an equal chance to survive? If so, how has this translated to how you respond to your neighbors or the children in your immediate world?

_____

_____

_____

A Fierce Response

Can a mother forget her nursing child? Can she feel no love for the child she has borne? But even if that were possible, I would not forget you!
Isaiah 49:15 NLT

Can a mother forget the infant at her breast, walk away from the baby she bore? But even if mothers forget, I'd never forget you—never.
Isaiah 49:15

We live in a day and time when even mothers have forgotten to love the ones they have nursed and carried within. Who ever imagined we would live in such a dark day that the natural affection and attachment of a mother would come into question? Sadly, it has. The fact that you've borne a child doesn't make you a mother. Likewise, the fact that you've never given birth does not disqualify you from motherhood. The response to the child determines the connection with the maternal.

We see this clearly illustrated in Solomon's court when he settles a dispute between two women who claim to be an infant's mother. Both women argued their case before the king, each claiming the boy as their own, but when the king provoked a response the truth was revealed.

After a moment the king said, "Bring me a sword."
They brought the sword to the king. Then he said, "Cut the living
baby in two—give half to one and half to the other."
The real mother of the living baby was overcome with emotion for her son
and said, "Oh no, master! Give her the whole baby alive; don't kill him!"
But the other one said, "If I can't have him,
you can't have him—cut away!"
The king gave his decision: "Give the living baby to the first woman.
Nobody is going to kill this baby. She is the real mother."

1 Kings 3:24-27

Both women had given birth, but only one was a real mother. Cutting something in half may be fair but at the same time unjust.

Worse followed. Refusing to know God, they soon didn't
know how to be human either—women didn't know how
to be women, men didn't know how to be men.

Romans 1:26

22 | How does this scripture speak to our day?

_____

_____

A loss of natural affection is not merely homosexuality here; it is a loss of all that makes humans created in the image of God. This translates to our sexuality as well as our maternal instincts. The women in Solomon's story were both prostitutes, but one had not lost her "natural" affection.

23 | How qualified must one be to care?

a. How do qualifications factor into our capacity and ability to respond?

Rescuing the Children

24 | What was your reaction to my story with the required-reading book?

25 | Are you involved with the material your children are reading in their formative years?

26 | Do you know pornographic images and input are highly destructive to the human sexuality?

Those images create an addiction cycle that is infused with shame and self-abuse that sooner or later transfers to another person.

Pornography begets victims both male and female. It is an addiction that can destroy young lives and cast them into realms of shadow and dark captivity.

27 | Have you spoken to your children, husband, or friends about the impact pornography has had on their lives?

_____

_____

_____

_____

28 | Were you affected by pornography?

_____

_____

_____

a. How did you deal with the imagery?

_____

_____

_____

29 | How can you constructively be involved in your area schools? As I understand it, even if you home school you can be involved.

_____

_____

_____

_____

It's Time to Hunt

In the hunt, the strength or weakness of one affects all. It is time we are honest with one another and look for ways to maximize strengths and minimize weaknesses.

This means telling one another where you need help. This means lending your strength.

Is your husband uninvolved and you need the support of friends? Is it hard for you to make time for fun? (This is one of my weaknesses.) Are you disorganized (yet another), etc.?

30 | List some areas of need or weakness in your life:

_____

_____

_____

_____

Isolating yourself from others or denying these weaknesses will not make them go away. There is strength and safety in the pride. There is weakness and risk outside the fold.

Let's be strong for one another. Let's construct rather than criticize. Let's give rather than hoard. Let's protect all rather than hide our own.

Take His Air

We all have weaknesses. We all have blind spots. Together they are swallowed up in a pride victory.

Stand united, singular in vision, contending for people's trust in the Message, the good news, not flinching or dodging in the slightest before the opposition. Your courage and unity will show them what they're up against: defeat for them, victory for you—and both because of God.

Philippians 1:27-28

Pride Play

Take note of the PROWESS among you! Use a ball of yarn or string, have one woman hold onto the end of the string and toss the ball to another sister and speak strength over an area of her personal prowess. The woman on the receiving end then holds onto her portion of the string and tosses the ball to another and speaks strength to her. Once you are finished, you have a connected group of highly strategic women!

Room for Reflection...

LIONESS LESSONS

- Hunts involve timing, camouflage, and proximity.
- God teaches us to hunt.
- When sisters grow up, they can potentially be the tightest relationship.
- You are part of writing this chapter.
- Justice requires energy and insight, and it must be guarded and protected.
- All the world's young deserve an equal chance to survive and play so they can thrive!
- Lionesses are the height of hunting prowess because they hunt together.

Pride Purpose

Giving birth does not make you a mother; responding to a child does.

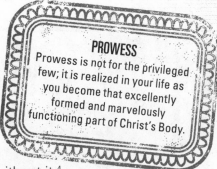

PROWESS

Prowess is not for the privileged few; it is realized in your life as you become that excellently formed and marvelously functioning part of Christ's Body.

FIERCE FACTS

* A lion's lifespan is 15 years in the wild or 13 years in captivity.[3]
* Most lions drink water daily if it is available but can go four or five days without it.[4]

Prayer Roar

I am ready to be excellently formed and marvelously functioning. Teach me to hunt. I am ready to grow up. Give me the energy and insight of heaven. Restore all of my healthy maternal affection that fear has twisted. I am ready to hunt with my sisters!

(1) *Sam Levenson Quotes* (http://www.brainyquote.com/quotes/authors/s/sam_levenson.html, retrieved 11-22-2010). (2) *Margaret Mead Quotes* (http://thinkexist.com/quotation/sister_is_prob-ably_the_most_competitive/12512.html, retrieved 11-22-2010). (3) "Out to Africa with Ellen & Paul," with permission from 45th Anniversary African Wildlife Foundation (http://www.outtoafri-ca.nl/animals/englion.html?zenden=2&subsoort_id=1&bestemming_id=1, Copyright: Paul Jans-sen, retrieved 11-11-2010). (4) Ibid.

IMPRESSIONS

LIONESSES LIVE IN THE LIGHT AND HUNT IN THE DARK 9

The wicked are edgy with guilt, ready to run off even when no one's after them; honest people are relaxed and confident, bold as lions.

Proverbs 28:1

It's an interesting combination: relaxed, confident, and bold! Like the lioness, we should express *all* of these—relaxed, bold confidence.

"I am what I am. I am powerful, focused, nurturing, highly skilled, playful, and deadly."

1 | How does this statement make you feel?

_____

_____

_____

_____

Like all women, the lioness is a collection of contradictions. Lionesses not only live in the light but they also live lightly. Nothing burdens the lions; they rise up, shake it off, and move only when necessary.

Lions are famous for lounging around in the golden sunlight and have been known to sleep up to 21 hours a day! Lionesses rest and relate unafraid in the full light of day. We likewise should live openly as our lives expand on ever-increasing levels. To live is to be in motion—growing, strengthening—as our connections multiply.

Living in the Light

You're out in the open now. The bright light of Christ makes your way plain. So no more stumbling around. Get on with it! The good, the right, the true—these are the actions appropriate for daylight hours. Figure out what will please Christ, and then do it.

Ephesians 5:8-10

It's time we move away from the shameful and shadowed realm. Do the good, the right, and the true. Notice the emphasis is on the "dos," not the "don'ts." We are children of light called to daylight actions even if we are in an environment that is dark.

And that's not all: We throw open our doors to God and discover at the same moment that he has already thrown open his door to us. We find ourselves standing where we always hoped we might stand—out in the wide open spaces of God's grace and glory, standing tall and shouting our praise.

Romans 5:2

We are the doorkeepers of our lives. We determine how open and closed the entrances and exits of our lives are. We regulate the traffic. Throw it wide to God! Then throw it wide for others by telling them about our big, generous God!

2 | Do you consider yourself an "open" person?

_____

_____

_____

3 | What doors have you shut that He is now asking you to open?

_____

_____

_____

4 | What are some ways you can live your life more openly?

_____

_____

_____

When all the doors are open, there is no stopping you! I recently heard a pastor say that if Satan can't stop you, he will push you. We should determine that we will not be pushed or burdened by him!

Are you tired? Worn out? Burned out on religion? Come to me. Get away with me and you'll recover your life. I'll show you how to take a real rest. Walk with me and work with me—watch how I do it. Learn the unforced rhythms of grace. I won't lay anything heavy or ill-fitting on you. Keep company with me and you'll learn to live freely and lightly.
Matthew 11:28-30

The answer to burnout is not inactivity but resting and learning to work with Him. In this way we cease any unattractive and exhaustive striving. It's time to take a walk with Him!

5 | Is there an area of life that is presently weighing on you?

_____

_____

_____

a. Is this an area in which you are not "keeping company" with Jesus?

_____

_____

6 | In the passage from Matthew 11, God invites us to walk, work, and watch. How can we do this?

_____

_____

_____

We're not keeping secrets, we're telling them; we're not hiding things,
we're bringing them out into the open.

Mark 4:22

7 | Is there something you are hiding that you long to release to the light?

_____

_____

_____

Recently a friend shared with me that someone knew about a private struggle from her past and they were now threatening to use it as blackmail against her. To break their sway and manipulation, she chose to bravely put her story out into the open. Don't let the enemy intimidate and blackmail you! Bring your secrets to His light. (If you didn't pray the prayer on page 161 of *Lioness Arising*, now would be a great time.)

Night Vision

We live in the light like lionesses; how do we hunt in the dark?

Lionesses have night vision; we too must acquire it. Lionesses can actually see in the dark by interpreting the light of their environment into vision. God has night vision too! If there was ever a time we needed this ability to see by a light within, it would be now.

I could ask the darkness to hide me and the light around me to become
night—but even in darkness I cannot hide from you. To you the night
shines as bright as day. Darkness and light are the same to you.

Psalm 139:11-12 NLT

Like our Father, we need to be able to see under all conditions.

8 | Do you find yourself uncomfortable and unable in dark conditions?

_____

_____

_____

9 | If we are the light bearers, why should we be uncomfortable?

_____

_____

_____

_____

10 | How can our vision remain unaffected by our environment?

_____

_____

_____

_____

If we are lit from within, our light level never changes and we face darkness head on and unafraid!

> ...that the God of our Lord Jesus Christ, the Father of glory,
> may give to you the spirit of wisdom and revelation in the knowledge
> of Him, the eyes of your understanding being enlightened;
> that you may know what is the hope of His calling.
>
> Ephesians 1:17-18 NKJV

He is the one who gives sight to the blind. **I want to challenge you to make Ephesians 1:17-18 your prayer for the next month.**

What you behold, you become.
What you see, you give expression to.
God, give us eyes to see as you do.

11 | What have you recently been beholding that you are now becoming?

Legend Lioness

"Don't call me an icon. I'm just a mother trying to help."
Princess Diana of Wales

_____

_____

a. What are you giving expression to?

_____

_____

_____

In these days, not only is it important for us to have ears that hear, but also eyes that see.

God said to Samuel, "Listen carefully. I'm getting ready to do something in Israel that is going to shake everyone up and get their attention."
1 Samuel 3:11

12 | Who was going to shake things up and get everyone's attention?

_____

God created the environment for the shake down; all Samuel had to do was flourish in the meantime. Even now God is saying, "Daughters, listen carefully. I'm going to do something in the earth that will shake things up and get the world's attention."

[In a season of darkness]...the boy Samuel was very much alive, growing up, blessed by God and popular with the people.
1 Samuel 2:26

13 | How does this description of *very much alive, maturing, blessed, and popular* compare with how the Church is described today?

_____

_____

_____

When I posted this description on Facebook and Twitter, people actually got angry and argued that we are not to be popular. Well, why shouldn't this be us: vibrantly alive, mature, evidently blessed by God, and popular with people?!

Would you like this to describe your life? Or would you rather be called almost-dead, immature, cursed by God, and unpopular?

If you are worried The Message translation is too liberal, the NKJV says, "Samuel grew in stature, and in favor both with the Lord and men!" And not only Samuel...what about our Jesus? He increased in wisdom, stature, and favor with God and men (Luke 2:52). So no more excuses for being grumpy and weird, then saying you're a prophet. Jesus is our example in everything. It was the religious leaders who were angry that Jesus was popular with the people.

14 | Have you had a religious, weird encounter with the prophetic that has put you off of it?

_____

_____

_____

_____

Jesus was never weird; He took God-wonder everywhere He went.

I give you permission to be wonderful but not weird! How did Jesus avoid weirdness? He remembered He represented His Father to a lost and dying world and only did what He saw His Father doing. We are to do likewise!

So Jesus explained himself at length. "I'm telling you this straight. The Son can't independently do a thing, only what he sees the Father doing. What the Father does, the Son does. The Father loves the Son and includes him in everything he is doing. But you haven't seen the half of it yet, for in the same way that the Father raises the dead and creates life, so does the Son. The Son gives life to anyone he chooses."

John 5:19-21

15 | Do you want in on this type of God-life?

_____

a. How much could Jesus do independently?

_____

In order to see some God-wonder, we need eyes that see. As His daughter you should want to see what your Father is doing. He tells us:

*"In the Last Days," God says, "I will pour out my Spirit on every kind of people: Your sons will **prophesy**, also your daughters; your young men will see visions, your old men dream dreams. When the time comes, I'll pour out my Spirit on those who serve me, men and women both, and they'll **prophesy**."*

Acts 2:17-18

You, lovely one, are prophetic by virtue of the timing of your birth! Prophets were called seers. The prophetic lends insight that is both visionary and farsighted. It has the capacity to span near and far. To be prophetic is to see what others miss: The disciples saw crowds; Jesus saw individuals.

16 | How does this change your perspective on the prophetic?

_____

_____

_____

_____

Through prophetic insight, answers are found where others only see problems. When nations were in trouble they historically turned to their king or their prophet.

17 | What was the consistent theme of the prophets?

_____

_____

_____

_____

*Before the Day of the Lord arrives, the Day tremendous and marvelous; and whoever calls out for help to me, God, will be **saved.***

Acts 2:20-21

There are individuals trapped in the dark waiting for you to see them and hear their cries. There are individuals who need you to close your eyes and see them when you pray!

Spirit
1. Strength: courage, character, will, force, fortitude, moral fiber, wisdom, determination, chutzpah, heart, mettle

18 | Give a biblical example of this:

_____

_____

_____

_____

Spirit
2. Inner self, life force, essence

19 | Give a biblical example of this:

_____

_____

_____

_____

Spirit
3. Ghost, phantom, ghoul, apparition

20 | Give a biblical example of this:

_____

_____

_____

_____

Spirit
4. General feeling, attitude, mood, tendency, atmosphere

21 | Give a biblical example of this:

_____

_____

_____

_____

22 | Drawing on the definitions of the word *spirit* and your examples, what might an outpouring look like?

_____

_____

_____

_____

23 | According to 1 Corinthians 14:4, what is the greatest gift that prophecy brings to the Church?

_____

_____

_____

Ultimately, God will have His way and reveal Himself.

He'll show us the way he works so we can live the way we're made.

Isaiah 2:3

I love this scripture because He promises to give us insight.

24 | What does Isaiah 2:3 speak to you?

_____

_____

_____

We were not made to walk around blinded by darkness. With a revelation of how He does things, we will learn to live the way we were made.

Visionary directives from Isaiah 49 and Romans 9:
1. Look up.
2. Look around.
3. Look well.
4. Look ahead.
5. Tell the truth.

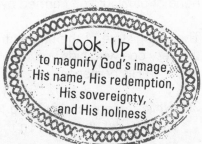

Look Up –
to magnify God's image,
His name, His redemption,
His sovereignty,
and His holiness

So let's ponder our Lord from another vantage. Let's revisit the imagery of Jesus from Revelation 1:12-17:

I turned and saw the voice. I saw a gold menorah with seven branches, and in the center, the Son of Man, in a robe and gold breastplate, hair a blizzard of white, eyes pouring fire-blaze, both feet furnace-fired bronze, His voice a cataract, right hand holding the Seven Stars, His mouth a sharp-biting sword, his face a perigee sun. I saw this and fainted dead at his feet.

I have highlighted some of the significant contrasts between Jesus the Son of Man on earth, and Jesus revealed as the Son of Man and the Son of God in heaven. Jesus was always robed, but on earth He had no breastplate of gold, which at once represents a triumphant, royal conqueror and warrior.

Then there is the hair that is a blizzard of white. If my hair is messed up, I might say it looks like I've been through a blizzard, but I would not call it a blizzard. Here in Colorado, a blizzard is a raging storm. Could it be that John saw a storm of sorts about the head of Jesus?

Next are His eyes, pouring out fire-blaze. All I can imagine is liquid lava or metal when it is so heated that it is liquid fire with the capacity to refine and consume.

The feet are the least frightening aspect. They are no longer sandaled; they are bronze like one who can walk through fire. His voice is a cataract, or massive waterfall, drowning out all other sounds. A hand that holds stars...my mind boggles. A mouth that is actually a sword...I also check out on this one. A face shining so brightly its radiance is as the sun at its zenith!

Is it any wonder John fainted? I am not suggesting we do likewise, but none of us would be harmed by a bit of trembling in awe.

This is a picture of the pageantry, posture, and power of our Lord. He is the very one who bids you to follow. Darkness would have no choice but to flee in His presence.

25 | While there is no doubting His majesty, is it hard for you to connect with our Jesus seated on the throne?

_____

_____

_____

_____

_____

I believe this connection is crucial because He is both the Son of Man and the Son of God, and He speaks to us from both positions.

26 | Which worship song helps you see Him in this posture?

_____

a. What portion or words in that song stirs this revelation in you?

_____

_____

_____

_____

27 | Do you want answers from the perspective of earth or heaven?

_____

a. Do you want to "act" according to the perspective of earth or heaven?

_____

⊠ HUNT QUEST ⊠

Set aside some time and play the song you mentioned either alone or, if time and technology permit, as a group. (In a group dynamic, pick the song most consistently chosen or known among the group.) Close your eyes, open your heart, and see Him—Son of God, Son of Man—ready to lead. Look for what He is showing you and write down what you see or hear in this time of worship. Then share it with the group.

_____

_____

_____

_____

_____

_____

Look Around –
to take the revelation of heaven and compare it with the reality of earth

We cannot help our world if we close our eyes and ears and hide from the pain that is around us.

28| What are some constructive ways you can become aware of need in your immediate world?

_____

_____

_____

_____

a. How can you raise your children's awareness?

_____

_____

_____

Look Well – needs to happen for health, healing, and redemption to occur

Looking well is to look beyond the problems and strategize a solution. It is finding holistic answers to systemic problems rather than just putting a bandage on them for a short while so we don't have to look at them.

29 | What is a root or core problem you might be able to bring solution, healing, or wellness to?

_____

_____

_____

_____

Look Ahead – the realization that our present choices live on

Here is where the need to be farsighted comes into play.

30 | What hard choices are you making today so that others outside your time will live well?

_____

_____

_____

_____

Tell the Truth – to not only speak truth, but to live it and send it into our future

But the hour cometh, and now is, when the true worshippers shall worship the Father in spirit and in truth: for the Father seeketh such to worship him. God is a Spirit: and they that worship him must worship him in spirit and in truth.

John 4:23-24 KJV

There is no Spirit-led worship outside of truth. He is Spirit, He is the Way, the Truth, and the Life. If truth is not proclaimed, no gathering is a safe place to worship. If truth is not lived, it is not a place of worship.

Make them holy—consecrated—with the truth; your word is consecrating truth. In the same way that you gave me a mission in the world, I give them a mission in the world. I'm consecrating myself for their sakes so they'll be truth-consecrated in their mission.

John 17:17-19

31 | According to John 17:17-19, what does truth have the power to do?

_____

_____

_____

_____

Pride Play

Which area in your city needs your light? Go on a night hunt. Find a time and place that works for your team and pray, greet, love, give, and be light to those who need it most! Look beyond the pain and bondage and shine light on the hidden hearts.

Room for Reflection...

_____

_____

_____

_____

_____

LIONESS LESSONS

- ✖ God wants us relaxed, bold, and confident.
- ✖ Our actions are to be appropriate for daylight hours: the good, right, and true.
- ✖ We are the doorkeepers of our lives.
- ✖ Burnout comes from working in our own strength.

- We are the *light* of the world. There is treasure waiting to be recovered from the domain of darkness.

- We are prophetic by virtue of timing.

- Prophetic people are like cats that see by the light within their eyes.

- We have permission to be vibrantly alive, mature, blessed, and popular!

- Weird is not wonderful.

- The outpouring of God's Spirit is more than we know.

- Spirit-led worship involves truth.

Pride Purpose

What you behold, you become.

PROWESS
We determine our light levels by how and what we choose to see in the world.

FIERCE FACTS

- Most cat species live a fundamentally solitary existence, but the lion is an exception. It has developed a social system based on teamwork, a division of labor within the pride, and an extended but closed family unit centered around a group of related females.[2]
- The lion is known as the king of beasts for its bravery and fighting skills.[3]

Prayer Roar

But you know all about it—the contempt, the abuse. I dare to believe that the luckless will get lucky someday in you. You won't let them down: orphans won't be orphans forever. Break the wicked right arms, break all the evil left arms. Search and destroy every sign of crime. God's grace and order wins; godlessness loses. The victim's faint pulse picks up; the hearts of the hopeless pump red blood as you put your ear to their lips. Orphans get parents, the homeless get homes. The reign of terror is over, the rule of the gang lords is ended.
[Psalm 10:14-18]

Together, let's hunt in the dark!

IMPRESSIONS

(1) *Quotations Book* (http://quotationsbook.com/quote/27778/, retrieved 11-15-2010). (2) "Out to Africa with Ellen & Paul," with permission from 45th Anniversary African Wildlife Foundation (http://www.outtoafrica.nl/animals/englion.html?zenden=2&subsoort_id=1&bestemming_id=1, Copyright: Paul Janssen, retrieved 11-11-2010). (3) *Interesting Facts About Lions* (http://EzineArticles.com/?expert=Omer_Ashraf, retrieved 11-15-2010).

IMPRESSIONS

WALKING WITH A LION 10

As I wrote the questions for this chapter, I was struck with the awareness that the key to this awakening in your life is very intimately tied to how you navigate them. I don't mean how you actually answer these questions on paper, but how you answer them with your life.

Far more important than your ability to hear from and connect with me is your personal ability to hear and connect with God.

There are paths I may never tread that you will walk in the company of our Lion. There are courses He may challenge you to take that I will never travel. He ultimately directs each of our lives. I never want to violate or limit this intimate place in your life. Likewise, you should never allow anyone to trespass this sacred ground.

In light of this charge, I want you to walk through these questions with sincerity and allow yourself to ponder, reflect on, and visualize life alongside our Lion.

If you are doing this with a group, remember there are no wrong answers—except dishonest ones. Esteem the honesty and vulnerability of one another so all who are present can truly grow.

1 | What are the areas of challenge you are currently navigating?

_____

_____

_____

2 | Where or what is God leading you into that you are afraid to follow?

_____

_____

_____

_____

Reread the passage from Matthew 16. I included verse 25 this time to give it a bit more context.

> Then Jesus went to work on his disciples. "Anyone who intends to come with me has to let me lead. You're not in the driver's seat; I am. Don't run from suffering; embrace it. Follow me and I'll show you how. Self-help is no help at all. Self-sacrifice is the way, my way, to finding yourself, your true self.
>
> Matthew 16:24-25

And,

> If any of you wants to be my follower, you must turn from your selfish ways, take up your cross, and follow me. If you try to hang on to your life, you will lose it. But if you give up your life for my sake, you will save it.
>
> Matthew 16:24-25 NLT

3 | When you read Matthew 16:24-25 in these versions, how do they expand on the way these three directives might look in your daily life?

"Let me lead" or "turn from your selfish ways":

_____

_____

"Embrace suffering" or "take up your cross":

_____

_____

"Follow me":

_____

_____

a. Is this directive a one-time altar dynamic, a progressive journey, or both?

_____

b. Are you (and we as the Church) doing all three? How or how not?

_____

_____

_____

4 | Do you wrestle with consistently knowing the voice of God? (I am not referring to specific direction such as a decision to be made, but His actual voice.)

_____

5 | Fix on a time in your memory when you *know* you heard God's voice. What did it sound like?

_____

_____

a. How did it come to you? (i.e., through the Word or a song, book, message, or quiet time)

_____

_____

b. How did you know it was God? Was it the way it made you feel (at peace, encouraged, burning heart)?

_____

_____

_____

c. Did its fruit, wisdom, or end result prove it over time?

_____

Walking by Faith

Let's revisit Hebrews 11:33...

> *By faith these people overthrew kingdoms, ruled with justice,*
> *and received what God had promised them.*
> (NLT)

And,

> *Through acts of faith, they toppled kingdoms, made justice work,*
> *took the promises for themselves.*

I have highlighted the words "these people" and "they" because I want you to note that the heroes' faith cited in Hebrews 11 were *people*—just like you and I are people. The difference is that they added faith into the mix of their humanity and did mighty exploits!

6 | What does an act of faith look like to you?

_____

_____

_____

7 | Tell of a time you acted in faith:

_____

_____

_____

8 | What do you think it means to take a promise for yourself?

_____

_____

a. What role does Scripture play in this?

_____

_____

9 | Though we are children of God, why aren't the promises of God auto-
matically set into motion in our lives?

_____

_____

_____

10 | Give an example of 2-3 promises...

a. You've previously appropriated in your life.

_____

_____

_____

b. You are presently laying hold of for others. (i.e. your husband,
children, church, leaders, friends)

_____

_____

_____

11 | What scriptures have you tied to these requests? (Give reference
only.) If you haven't bound them to any scriptures, then now would be
a great time to do so.

_____

_____

_____

_____

12 | What kingdom(s) would you like to see topple through an act of faith?

13 | What areas of injustice do you want to address?

14 | What doubts do you battle on a regular basis?

An act of faith produces an action, or an area of activity, in our lives.

In the case of Abraham and Sarah, it meant leaving behind all that was known and familiar to step into the unknown and unfamiliar.

15 | Do you think the unknown and unfamiliar is where we usually meet God?

16 | What is more appealing to you...a map or a mystery?

a. Which has more potential to develop your character, life skills, and intuition?

17 | What do you actually say to friends who are feeling overwhelmed by what God has set before them?

_____

_____

_____

_____

a. Do you add faith to them, or do you add in caution and perhaps an element of fear because you are afraid for them? (To answer this question, recall the last time a conversation like this transpired. What was your actual response?)

_____

_____

_____

_____

_____

_____

> *"It is the greatest of all mistakes to do nothing because you can only do little – do what you can."*
> Sydney Smith

Don't Hold Back

This is how heaven sees you:

> *God told me, "Don't say, 'I'm only a boy.' I'll tell you where to go and you'll go there. I'll tell you what to say and you'll say it. Don't be afraid of a soul. I'll be right there, looking after you." God's Decree. God reached out, touched my mouth, and said, "Look! I've just put my words in your mouth—hand-delivered!"*
> Jeremiah 1:7-9

18 | If God told Jeremiah not to make his age an issue, do you believe your age is an issue for God?

_____

19 | Can any of us be too young or old for the direction and protection of God?

_____

20 | What about gender? Do you believe God would say to you, "Don't say, 'I'm only a girl, woman, mother, grandmother?'"

_____

We only argue about these details when we have forgotten the point of this interaction. It was not about Jeremiah. This interchange was about God's directives—where to go, what to say, and ultimately Jeremiah's obedience—"you'll say it!"

There seems to be a parallel between this and the commission of Jesus to His disciples in Matthew 28:18-20:

> *Jesus, undeterred, went right ahead and gave his charge: "God authorized and commanded me to commission you: Go out and train everyone you meet, far and near, in this way of life, marking them by baptism in the threefold name: Father, Son, and Holy Spirit. Then instruct them in the practice of all I have commanded you. I'll be with you as you do this, day after day after day, right up to the end of the age."*
>
> Matthew 28:18-20

Jesus' command was to train everyone they met. Surely they met women, young and old. What were they to train and instruct them in? The practice of all He'd commanded—His way of life.

21 | How did Jesus conduct His life?

_____

_____

_____

_____

Trust Your Lion Encounters

Reread the excerpt from Prince Caspian found on page 196 of *Lioness Arising.*

22 | How did you feel when you read Lucy's interaction with her brothers and sister?

_____

_____

_____

   a. Have you ever felt that you were unable to communicate what you saw to another?

     _____

   b. What troubled or frustrated you the most?

     _____

     _____

I think the most frustrating element here is that Lucy's integrity and ability to see and rightly know was questioned.

23 | Was there a time when you likewise followed behind others weeping because you felt you had no other choice? Or did you choose a different course?

_____

_____

_____

In the course of life there are frequent and repeated opportunities for misunderstanding and to be misunderstood. If these are not handled well, bitterness and rejection can enter our soul and taint our words and choices. The only way to avoid this is to stop blaming others and take responsibility for our own choices.

We are all tempted to echo Lucy's words and declare, "But it wasn't my fault!"

We all have fault. Blame doesn't fly in the presence of our Lion. At His feet we see what we missed during the course of our day.

24 | Lovely lioness, is there any area of life or relationship that you have continually declared justification over?

_____

_____

If so, let's look it in the eye and own our part; then we can move on in our our journey to release others. This does not have to be a big deal, but it needs to happen. Let's take ownership and lay all of it at His feet.

Pause—Whisper it—Write a word, name, or symbol to capture it. Close your eyes and repeat these words in prayer:

> Heavenly Father,
> It doesn't matter. I forgive and release this situation (or person). No longer will I allow it (or him/her) to hold me back. Amen.

Lovely lioness, God is setting you up for an adventure. You cannot fail if you follow Him. No matter how horrid your adventure has been up to this point, there is triumph in your future.

You Are a Lioness

Reread the excerpt on the top of page 200 in _Lioness Arising_.

25 | What was your response to this declaration?
"Now you are a lioness," said Aslan. "And now all Narnia will be renewed."

_____

_____

_____

It is an awesome realization that our response has the potential to renew others.

26 | Do you believe that times of intimacy during which we hide our face in Him can bring lion-strength?

_____

a. When was the last time this happened with you and what was the result?

_____

_____

_____

b. Are you also willing to say you are ready even if you are unsure where He will take you?

_____

The Courage to Make a Difference

It is time we remembered that where we are going is not where we have been. A new horizon and battlefield are spread before us.

> _...according to the prophecies previously made concerning you, that by them you may wage the good warfare._
> 1 Timothy 1:18 NKJV

27 | Pause and remember some of the prophecies or promises that have been spoken over your life. These could be things whispered to you by God or declared over you by leaders. One is not less than the other. So without disqualifying or doubting, write the essence of them here:

_____

_____

_____

_____

According to the scripture from 1 Timothy, these are more than a wish. These are words of life, which have the potential to be weapons of light and hope.

28 | If you truly believe this, how will your approach to them change?

_____

_____

_____

a. How are you now wielding them?

_____

_____

_____

⊠ HUNT QUEST ⊠

Legend Lioness

"The burden that has fallen upon me maketh me amazed."[2]

Queen Elizabeth I

This quote proves we choose our response to enormous weights of responsibility and opposition. Of course you do not need to rule a nation to feel overwhelmed. You can be a stay-at-home mother and discover an amazing load has been added to your life.

Not long ago I posted a comment on Twitter and Facebook from one of my husband's sermons that "faithful people multiply what is entrusted to them."

A lovely stay-at-home mother, who was already feeling overwhelmed, reacted and declared herself useless in this season of raising young ones. When I reminded her that training, loving, and caring for children is multiplication of the best sort, she felt empowered just by the change of perspective.

29 | What areas of life are looming large and presently threatening to overwhelm you?

_____

_____

_____

a. Write down your new perspective or response to these areas or challenges.

_____

_____

_____

_____

30 | What inspires you most about Queen Elizabeth?

_____

_____

_____

Another thing I discovered as I studied her life was that she did not tolerate excuses. She did not make them for herself or allow them for her subjects. I love this. Because she did not make excuses, she was always positioned on the offensive and well-able to execute a course of action.

_____

Elizabeth is a legend lioness. History has remembered her well, even if her own time period was unkind.

31 | Who in your world is a present-day legend lioness?

_____

_____

_____

_____

Legend Lioness

"Though God hath raised me high, yet this I count the glory of my Crown, that I have reigned with your loves. ... I have ever used to set the last Judgement Day before mine eyes and so to rule as I shall be judged to answer before a higher judge."[3]

Queen Elizabeth I, Golden Speech of 1601

32 | What do you want to be remembered for?

_____

_____

_____

Are you ready to be amazed by God? Are you ready to be amazing? The best path of wonder is in a revelation of Him.

33 | So lovely lioness sisters, what do you see?

_____

_____

_____

34 | What are you hearing?

_____

_____

_____

35 | What amazing course is He inviting you to walk with Him?

_____

_____

_____

Pride Play

Are you holding back on something you feel you're supposed to do? Where do you need victory? As a group of lioness sisters, go before the Lion of the Tribe of Judah in prayer. Allow Him to stir strength and wonder within!

Room for Reflection...

_____

_____

_____

LIONESS LESSONS

- ▨ Never allow anyone to trespass your sacred ground.

- ▨ Fear gives awful counsel.

- ▨ Laying blame and making excuses doesn't work with our Lion.

- ▨ Our response has the potential to renew others.

Pride Purpose

Burdens can be amazing.

PROWESS
Faith speaks in your actions.

FIERCE FACTS

- Adult lions weigh 330 to 500 pounds, lionesses 265 to 400 pounds. Height is 4 feet (males) to 3.5 feet (females). Length is 4.5 to 8.25 feet.[4]
- A male lion is referred to as a lion or tom. A female lion is referred to as a she-lion or lioness. The name of offspring is a cub, whelp, or lionet.[5]

Prayer Roar

Forgive me for the times I have said, "I'm only..." in response to an invitation to adventure. I want Your mystery, not my map. Forgive me for the times I have blamed others and disobeyed You. Where You choose to lead, I will follow. I am ready to rise up a lioness unafraid and multiply Your life in the lives of others.

(1) *Quotations about Helping and Making a Difference* (http://www.quotegarden.com/helping. html, retrieved 11-22-2010). (2) Alan Axelrod, *Elizabeth I, CEO: Strategic Lessons from the Leader Who Built an Empire* (Paramus, NJ: Prentice Hall, 2000), p. 6. (3) *Elizabeth I Quotes* (http://www. great-quotes.com/quote/36037, retrieved 11-22-2010). (4) *The Jungle Store* (http://www.thejun- glestore.com/Lion-Facts, retrieved 11-11-2010). (5) *Facts about Lions* (http://www.facts-about. org.uk/animals-lions.htm, retrieved 11-11-2010).

IMPRESSIONS

FROM A WHISPER TO A ROAR 11

"Prayer is exhaling the spirit of man and inhaling the spirit of God."[1]
Edwin Keith

Our lives should be a constant cycle of emptying ourselves so we may be filled again. The response to the amazing time, entrustment, and destiny set before us should be humility, which gives birth to prayer.

Humility is the WHISPER that prayer transforms to a ROAR.

You, lovely lioness sister, have the capacity to roar, but like Simba in *The Lion King*, you must realize it. Let's review again how the lion's posture changes so it can produce a roar.

1. It rises.
2. It shakes or rouses itself.
3. It drops its head.
4. It inhales until it reaches capacity.
5. It releases what is within.
6. It listens for a response.
7. It repeats all the steps above until it knows it is heard.

I think we have seen these steps on our journey through this book. First we realized God was asking us to rise up and recover our feet. Then it was time to release ourselves from the lethargy of our day to day. When the realization of the conditions that have arisen in our season of apathy hit us, we were humbled to repentance. This means we were emptied of our religious selves and positioned to be filled by what God alone can provide. As we are truly filled with His life and light, then we have something to release to others. We lift our voices first in a whisper, but when the whisper is echoed, we raise the volume.

"Don't pray for lighter burdens, but for stronger backs."
Anonymous

We will change when we learn to pray for strength rather than relief! This is the very posture change we all need. When I observed the lions truly roaring, I saw that it commanded their whole being. I have a picture on my desk of a lion roaring; even its eyes are closed to give focus to its sound. What's before us will command the strength and focus of both our individual and corporate church being.

1 | When you read the "anonymous" quote above, how does it fit in with your current prayers?

_____

_____

_____

I fear too often and too many people pray that their load will be lightened. I know in the past I prayed God would make the way easier, stop the attack, and turn things in my favor. But now I pray for strength.

2 | Why is it important that our prayers change?

_____

_____

_____

Our roar or declaration must be more than a sound. It must be a divine merger of arresting words, deeds, and actions of faith.

3 | How did Jesus arrest with words?

_____

_____

_____

a. What deeds did He suggest for those who follow Him?

_____

_____

The intangibles of faith, hope, and love must become tangible in our individual lives and expressed in a unified response to the world's needs and God's love!

> As we exemplify our Lion, the world will hear His roar!

4 | Give an example of what each of these would look like if tangible:

Faith:

_____

_____

Hope:

_____

_____

Love:

_____

_____

God is increasing the volume!

God roars like a lion from high heaven;
thunder rolls out from his holy dwelling.

Jeremiah 25:30

And again He declares:

The people will end up following God. I will roar like a lion—Oh, how
I'll roar! My frightened children will come running from the west.

Hosea 11:10

5 | What new imagery of God do these scriptures awaken in you?

_____

_____

_____

_____

The frightened children will run to their roaring God, but those who are not His will flee in terror. It appears God begins with a whisper—He whispered life into Adam—but the finale is a roar.

It Begins with a Whisper

6 | Look up the definition for the word *whisper* and write it here:

_____

_____

_____

7 | Do you think we miss the voice of God because, like Elijah, we are looking for something loud and obvious?

_____

_____

8 | When was the last time God whispered something to you?

_____

_____

_____

a. Did He whisper to you as you read?

_____

b. What did He whisper?

_____

_____

_____

9 | How have you seen the statement, "Everything out loud begins with a whisper" played out in your life?

_____

_____

_____

_____

_____

_____

> *"It is better in prayer to have a heart without words than words without a heart."*[2]
> Mahatma Gandhi

10 | Do you whisper your prayers?

_____

_____

Be still, and know that I am God! I will be honored by every nation. I will be honored throughout the world.
Psalm 46:10 NLT

11 | Do you find this "still knowing" difficult?

_____

_____

_____

a. What do you do or where do you go to still yourself?

_____

_____

_____

12 | What God-whisper have you felt stirring within you?

_____

_____

_____

There are plenty of prophets and kings who would have given their right arm to see what you are seeing but never got so much as a glimpse, to hear what you are hearing but never got so much as a whisper.

Luke 10:24

13 | Why did those who were watching miss the obvious?

_____

_____

_____

_____

a. What warning does this bring to us?

_____

_____

_____

From a Whisper to a Shout

14 | Define *shout*:

_____

_____

_____

_____

Legend Lioness

"The God-whisper has become a shout."[3]

Bobbie Houston, Hillsong Church

15 | In the context of what God is doing in and among His daughters, what was your reaction to Bobbie's profound statement?

_____

_____

_____

_____

What I whisper in your ear, shout from the housetops for all to hear!
Matthew 10:27 NLT

What God begins in a whisper, we have the privilege of ending with a shout!

16 | What is the Holy Spirit whispering in your ear that He is asking you to proclaim out loud?

_____

_____

_____

_____

The whisper of God is so tantalizing it can frighten.
So provocative it can isolate in its aftermath.
So powerful that, once set into motion, it is impossible to stop.
[page 211]

17 | Why is a whisper often more intriguing than out-loud conversation?

_____

_____

_____

_____

_____

18 | In your experience, what is harder to stop—a whisper or a statement?

_____

a. Why do you think this is?

_____

_____

_____

_____

Thunder crashes and rumbles in the skies. Listen! It's God raising his voice! By his power he stills sea storms, by his wisdom he tames sea monsters. With one breath he clears the sky, with one finger he crushes the sea serpent. And this is only the beginning, a mere whisper of his rule. Whatever would we do if he really raised his voice!

Job 26:11-14

Fortunately, we know the answer to that final statement: We will come running! But we do need to wonder at the might of "a mere whisper of his rule."

19 | What reaction does this passage inspire in you?

_____

_____

_____

Legend Lioness

"Prayer lays hold of God's plan and becomes the link between His will and its accomplishment on earth. Amazing things happen, and we are given the privilege of being the channels of the Holy Spirit's prayer."[4]

Elisabeth Elliot, author and speaker, spent two years as a missionary to the Auca people (now known as Huaorani) of eastern Ecuador after her husband was killed while attempting to make missionary contact with them

20 | What areas of life have been made uncomfortable for you because God has whispered life, freedom, wildness, beauty, and value into them?

_____

_____

_____

_____

_____

_____

_____

21 | What did Mary do with her God-whisper?

_____

_____

_____

    a. Is it sometimes best to remain quiet until we give birth?

_____

_____

22 | How do you treasure, record, or store up what God whispers to you?

_____

_____

Live the Whisper Out Loud

"None of us will ever accomplish anything excellent or commanding except when he listens to this whisper which is heard by him alone."[5]

Ralph Waldo Emerson

23 | What excellent, commanding thing is God whispering to you?

_____

_____

_____

We hear alone only to discover later that others have likewise heard. This is how all the puzzle pieces begin to fit together.

But you belong. The Holy One anointed you, and you all know it. I haven't been writing this to tell you something you don't know, but to confirm the truth you do know, and to remind you that the truth doesn't breed lies.

1 John 2:20-21

Lovely one, you belong—because you belong to Him.

I have learned that to truly belong there must be a knowing of truth. No one else can realize truth for us. John explained to his brothers and sisters in Christ that he was only confirming what they already knew within.

> Don't shout. In fact, don't even speak—not so much as a whisper until you hear me say, "Shout!"—then shout away!
>
> Joshua 6:10

A whisper isolates us for a season so it can connect us later. When you were born again, the whisper told you there was something more to life. You searched for something more and discovered a life in God. With your rebirth you are no longer part of an isolated family; you become part of God's body.

Timing is crucial; we live in strategic and perilous times. God is secretly surrounding some things, and when the time is right, He will bring them down with a shout!

24 | What areas is God asking you to silently encircle or surround with prayer?

_____

_____

_____

> "There is a vast difference between saying prayers and praying."
> Anonymous

True prayer can actually happen without audible or intelligible words. It is an expression of the inexpressible. It is in its purest form when it is authored by the Spirit of God—*Thy kingdom come, Thy will be done*—allowing His will to trump ours.

25 | What is your favorite part of the Lord's Prayer and why?

_____

_____

_____

a. Do you think the Lord's Prayer was meant to be a pattern or ritual?

_____

_____

_____

> *Like a woman having a baby, writhing in distress,*
> *screaming her pain as the baby is being born.*
>
> Isaiah 26:17

I remember when I gave birth to my sons I heard myself make a sound I could not have authored. It came from deep within me and was completely unexpected, but the labor and delivery nurses knew by the utterance that a life was about to be brought forth. How did they know? Their ears were trained to listen for the sound of travail.

In my spirit I sense not only the volume rising but also the source of sound shifting as we begin to labor with God. In labor you don't only scream or groan—you push and work.

26 | If you've had a baby, did you have a similar experience?

_____

_____

_____

Hurt women screaming their pain is not an answer. Expectant women gathering in prayer to ease the pain of others (male and female) is an answer.

Let's bring forth life from the pain of our labor. Let's redeem the labor, the prejudice, and the pain to birth strong, vibrant sons and daughters!

27 | What are the areas of present or past pain in your life that could be transformed and redeemed to birth life and hope for others?

_____

_____

_____

When the Shout Becomes a Roar

28 | Define *roar:*

_____

_____

_____

_____

> *"Pray as though everything depended on God. Work as though everything depended on you."*[6]
>
> St. Augustine

29 | If you believe this, list some ways it changes how you:

Pray

_____

_____

_____

_____

Work

_____

_____

_____

As the book of James tells us, faith without works is dead! Prayer releases our fear and worry so that God can get involved; then our actions (or acts of faith) express that we believe He is backing us.

⊞ HUNT QUEST ⊞

"I prayed for twenty years but received no answer until I prayed with my legs."[7]

Frederick Douglass, escaped slave

When Frederick rose up and found his feet, he married his actions to his faith. Because he set his prayers into motion, other slaves were freed.

Likewise, lioness sisters, we must pray with our hands, feet, mouths, finances, possessions, creativity, and life choices.

30 | What is one way you could even now set your prayers in motion?

_____

_____

_____

_____

_____

_____

"I was not the lion, but it fell to me to give the lion's roar."[8]
Winston Churchill

When I read this, I wondered, *Could there be a quote more perfect for our time?* We are not "the Lion"; He alone has that preeminence. But it has fallen to us to release His roar. So let's review the "why" behind the lion's roar...

The lion's roar:
1. Proclaims and protects territory: "I am alert, powerful, and present."
2. Intimidates enemies with a declaration that harassment will not be tolerated.
3. Sets boundaries for would-be invaders.
4. Declares allegiances and alliances by locating members of the pride: "Here I am; where are you?"
5. Reveals strength, age, and characteristics of the roaring lion.

The lioness's roar:
1. Protects her young.
2. Validates her relationship with members of the pride.
3. Calls in lost and wandering cubs.
4. Creates an ambush.
5. Attracts her mate.

Reasons *we* should roar:
1. To declare His domain.
2. To affirm our allegiance.
3. To raise a battle cry.
4. To call in the lost and wandering.
5. To check the movement of trespassers, enemies, and thieves.
6. To protect our young from death and destruction.
7. Because we will not face the darkness in silence.

Again, I want to emphasize that I believe our roar is first and foremost a collective expression of prayer, merged with corresponding action, motivated by love, expressed through faith, which ultimately results in bringing hope to the hopeless.

In the book of Acts we see the power of this type of collective prayer:

*And now, Lord, behold their threatenings: and grant unto thy servants, that with all boldness they may speak thy word, by stretching forth thine hand to heal; and that signs and wonders may be done by the name of thy holy child Jesus. And when they had prayed, the place was **shaken** where they were assembled together; and they were all **filled** with the Holy Ghost, and they spake the word of God with **boldness.***

Acts 4:29-31 KJV

What does this type of prayer yield?
1. The place of assembly was shaken.
2. All were filled with the Holy Ghost.
3. The Word of God was spoken with boldness.

It is my prayer that this message has left you with a hunger to be shaken, filled, and bold. This type of empowerment seems reserved for those who choose to assemble together.

31 | Name 2 other times this happened in the Bible.

_____

_____

_____

a. What was the result?

_____

_____

_____

By yourself you're unprotected. With a friend you can face the worst. Can you round up a third? A three-stranded rope isn't easily snapped.

Ecclesiastes 4:12

We are also promised:

Take this most seriously: A yes on earth is yes in heaven; a no on earth is no in heaven. What you say to one another is eternal. I mean this. When two of you get together on anything at all on earth and make a prayer of it, my Father in heaven goes into action. And when two or three of you are together because of me, you can be sure that I'll be there.

Matthew 18:18-20

Do we pray like we truly believe this? I must admit I don't. But in all honesty, I pray alone. I wonder what might happen if my prayers were joined with another's.

Prayer Roars

Let's review why we must no longer neglect the gathering or underestimate the power of our concert of prayer.

> *"No one is a firmer believer in the power of prayer than the devil; not that he practices it, but he suffers from it."[9]*
> Guy H. King

32 | From pages 220 and 221 in *Lioness Arising*, list 4 reasons why we should roar our prayers:

1. _____

2. _____

3. _____

4. _____

As God continues to relate us, we will be less vulnerable and afraid. Not only should we gather in groups of two or more but our prayers are best woven into three-fold cords:

> *Jesus said, "Love the Lord your God with all your passion and prayer and intelligence."*
> Matthew 22:37

And,

> *Jesus said unto him, Thou shalt love the Lord thy God with all thy heart, and with all thy soul, and with all thy mind.*
> Matthew 22:37 KJV

I want to combine these two versions:

> Jesus said, "Love the Lord your God with all your passionate heart and with all your soul's prayer and your mind's intelligence."

This is how we love our God. We consecrate our entire being and give expression to His worship and purpose. This can happen through passionate, intelligent prayers.

> *Everything in the world is about to be wrapped up, so take nothing for granted. Stay wide-awake in prayer.*
> 1 Peter 4:7

In prayer God releases strategies and thwarts the plans of the enemy. In prayer we are changed so that we can see heaven invade earth through our offered lives.

> *"Prayer does not change God, but it changes him who prays."[10]*
> Søren Kierkegaard

It begins with our whisper of prayer and then moves into words spoken in conversation. As conversation is unified in purpose, the shout is born. As the shout rises collectively, it becomes a roar. There is no true beginning without prayer.

So, lovely ones, you need to pray first so you can become all you were destined to be. This world needs your prayers. Will you commit to this?

"Rise like Lions after slumber
In unvanquishable number,
Shake your chains to earth like dew
Which in sleep had fallen on you—
Ye are many—they are few."

Percy Bysshe Shelley

There are more with us than with them. If God is for us, who can be against us?

For information on how to remain connected:
www.LionessArising.com
www.facebook.com/LionessArising

Lionesses, lift your voices!

Pride Play

Now that great fierceness has been stirred within you, change your posture. Play a couple of your favorite worship songs, kneel before the God of heaven and allow Him to fill you with a fresh infilling of the Spirit. I believe that through this act humility, your capacity will be greatly enlarged.

Room for Reflection...

_____

_____

_____

_____

_____

_____

_____

_____

LIONESS LESSONS

- Humility is the WHISPER that prayer transforms to a ROAR.
- Our roar or declaration must be more than a sound. It must be a divine merger of arresting words, deeds, and actions of faith.
- What God begins in a whisper, we have the privilege of ending with a shout!
- Prayer is in its purest form when it is authored by the Spirit of God—*Thy kingdom come, Thy will be done*—allowing His will to trump ours.
- We must pray with our hands, feet, mouths, finances, possessions, creativity, and life choices.

Pride Purpose

We love our God by consecrating our entire being and giving expression to His worship and purpose.

PROWESS

Our roar is first and foremost a collective expression of prayer, merged with corresponding action, motivated by love, expressed through faith, which ultimately results in bringing hope to the hopeless.

Legend Lioness

"It is for us to pray not for tasks equal to our powers, but for powers equal to our tasks, to go forward with a great desire forever beating at the door of our hearts as we travel toward our distant goal."[14]

Helen Keller

FIERCE FACTS

- Though lions used to live in most parts of Africa, they are now found only in the south Sahara desert and in parts of southern and eastern Africa. Historically, in addition to Africa, lions were found from Greece through the Middle East to northern India.[12]
- Lion cubs weigh about 3 pounds at birth. By age 2 they are good hunters.[13]

Prayer Roar

Pray, pray, pray!

IMPRESSIONS

(1) *Edwin Keith Quotes* (http://thinkexist.com/quotation/prayer_is_exhaling_the_spirit_of_man_ and_inhaling/204483.html, retrieved 11-30-2010). (2) *Mahatma Ghandi Quotes* (http://thinkexist. com/quotation/prayer_is_not_asking-it_is_a_longing_of_the_soul/148514.html, retrieved 11-15-2010). (3) Lisa Bevere, *Lioness Arising* (Colorado Springs, CO: Waterbrook Press, 2010) p. 210. (4) *Great Quotes on Prayer* (http://powertochange.com/experience/spiritual-growth/prayer-quotes/, retrieved 11-15-2010). (5) *Ralph Waldo Emerson Quotes* (http://thinkexist.com/quotation/ none_of_us_will_ever_accomplish_anything/223531.html, retrieved 11-15-2010). (6) *St. Augus-tine Quotes* (http://thinkexist.com/quotation/pray_as_though_everything_depended_on_god-work_as/149654.html, retrieved 11-15-2010). (7) *Frederick Douglass Quotes* (http://thinkexist. com/quotation/i_prayed_for_twenty_years_but_received_no_answer/205929.html, retrieved 11-15-2010). (8) *Quotations Book* (http://quotationsbook.com/quote/22801/, retrieved 11-15-2010). (9) *Guy H. King Quotes* (http://thinkexist.com/quotation/no_one_is_a_firmer_believer_in_the_ power_of/206780.html, retrieved 11-30-2010). (10) *Finest Quotes* (http://www.finestquotes. com/select_quote-category-Prayer-page-0.htm, retrieved 11-15-2010). (11) See note 3, p. 222. (12) *African Lion Facts* (http://www.defenders.org/wildlife_and_habitat/wildlife/lion.php, retrieved 12-6-2010). (13) Ibid. (14) *Helen Keller Quotes* (http://www.brainyquote.com/quotes/authors/h/ helen_keller.html, retrieved 11-15-2010).

IMPRESSIONS

LIONESS
ARISING
CURRICULUM

Curriculum Includes:

- 8 Video Sessions on 3 DVDs (30 minutes each)
- 8 Audio Sessions on 4 CDs (30 minutes each)
- *Lioness Arising* hardcover book
- Safari Guide
- Promotional materials to help gather groups

Churches & Pastors -

Local churches are the passion and heart of this ministry. Our Church Relations team connects with pastors, churches, and ministry leaders worldwide. It is their joy and honor to encourage leaders, pray for churches, provide life-transforming resources, and build authentic relationships.

UNITED STATES	AUSTRALIA	UNITED KINGDOM
1-800-648-1477	1-300-650-577	0800-9808-933

Curriculum Includes:

- 8 sessions on 3 DVDs and 4 CDs (30 minutes each)
- Hardcover book
- *Fencing Manual* study guide
- Sword necklace
- Promotional materials

What if you discovered you have been entrusted with an invisible, invincible, and incorruptible weapon? Would you use it? Move beyond study and begin to wield the Word of God. If there ever was a time for women to be armed, it's now.

nurure

Give and Get What You Need to Flourish

Curriculum Includes:

- 7 Sessions on 3 DVDs & 3 CDs (30 minutes each)
- *Nurture* Book
- Devotional Workbook
- Encouraging Videos from 17 international leaders
- Promotional Materials
- Cross Necklace: Adjustable 16-18 inch Genuine Swarovski Crystal Necklace

Nurture is what you need to give and get! As God's daughters, it is our season to flourish! This curriculum positions you to make connections, write your life, reclaim your feminine intuition, strengthen your family, and find your place as the world-changer God has destined you to be.

Beautiful Daughter, this world needs you, so find your voice and bring your strength!

Fight Like *a Girl*
The Power of Being a Woman
You are an answer, not a problem.

Curriculum Includes:

- 12 Video Sessions on 4 DVDs (30 minutes each)
- *Fight Like a Girl* Book
- Devotional Workbook
- Promotional Materials & Bookmark
- Makeup Bag
- Bracelet – Genuine Swarovski Austrian Crystal

In *Fight Like a Girl*, Lisa challenges the status quo that a woman needs to fit into the role of a man, and she leads you in the truth of what it means to be a woman. Discover how to express your God-given strengths and fulfill your role in the community, workplace, home, and church. This curriculum will encourage you to find your true potential and realize you are an answer and not a problem.

Curriculum Includes:

- 4 Video Sessions & Bonus Q&A on 2 DVDs (50-60 minutes each)
- Best-selling Book
- Devotional Workbook
- Promotional Materials

Don't believe the lie—sexual purity isn't about rules...it's about freedom and power. It is time to take back what we've cheaply given away. This kit is for women of all ages who long for a greater intimacy with Jesus and need to embrace God's healing and restoring love.

"I'm 15, and through your kit my nightmare has been turned back to a dream!"

additional RESOURCES

Life Without Limits – DVD

It is definitely no longer about us, but about Him! God is calling a generation of women who are willing to take risks and go out over their heads in Him. Women brave enough to trust Him with every area of their life. He is watching for wild women who will be reckless in both their abandonment to God and their commitment to obedience. It is time to embrace His freedom in every area. This powerful and dynamic video was recorded at a women's mentoring conference and will empower you in these crucial areas:

- Completing versus competing
- Making your marriage a place of power
- Refining and defining your motivation
- Harnessing your power of influence
- Answering the mandate

Healing for the Angry Heart – 4 CD SET

In *Healing for the Angry Heart*, author Lisa Bevere provides practical, biblical insights to help you deal with the past and move forward in your life.

In this course, Lisa discusses:

- Her Anger Issues
- The Power of Confession
- Stopping Anger Before It Gets Out of Hand
- Letting It Go
- Putting It Into Practice
- Anger and Depression
- Anger and Fear

The Power of Two with One Heart – CD

God never intended our marriages to be something we endure, but a beautiful and exciting haven where both the man and woman flourish.

In *The Power of Two with One Heart*, Lisa calls out to both men and women to see God's original plan for marriage and to take back what has been lost. When we embrace our roles and lend our strengths, it is then the restoration can begin.

With God, it's always been about one man, one woman, one heart.

Extreme Makeover – 2 CD SET

Makeovers of every kind are the current craze. Not only are faces and bodies being hauled over, but everything is subject to this before-and-after experimentation. People just can't seem to get enough, and rather than judging, the church needs to ask the all-important question...Why? I believe it is because we are all desperate for change!

It's Time – CD

For too long we have had the attitude, "It's my turn!" But when God begins to pour out His spirit, it is nobody's turn; it becomes everybody's time. It is time for God's gifts in His body to come forth. The Father is gifting men and women alike to shine in each and every realm of life. Discover what He has placed in your hand and join the dance of a lifetime.